T0368318

This workbook comes with two CDs. To receive the accompanying CD's,
please contact the author at theresa@accent-professional.com.

This book is sold subject to the condition that it shall not, by way of trade or otherwise, be lent, resold, hired out, or otherwise circulated without the publisher's prior consent in any form of binding or cover other than that in which it is published and without a similar condition including this condition being imposed on the subsequent purchaser.

Tongue Twisters, Rhymes, and Songs to Improve Your English Pronunciation

Theresa M. Bareither, SLP
Speech-Language Pathologist

authorHOUSE®

AuthorHouse™ LLC
1663 Liberty Drive, Suite 200
Bloomington, IN 47403
www.authorhouse.com
Phone: 1-800-839-8640

©2011 Theresa Bareither. All rights reserved.

No part of this book may be reproduced, stored in a retrieval system, or transmitted by any means without the written permission of the author.

Published by AuthorHouse   06/24/2013

ISBN: 978-1-4343-3419-0 (sc)
ISBN: 978-1-4685-6594-2 (e)

This book is printed on acid-free paper.

Table of Contents

Introduction

Who are you, and why are you reading this book?

Okay. You are living and working in the United States, or perhaps you are living and working in your home country using English on a daily basis for business. You have basic English language fluency. I admire you because it has been a dream of mine to be able to speak another language—any language—as well as you speak English.

But darn it! Don't you get a little tired of those funny looks? Doesn't it get annoying to hear, "Could you repeat that please?"

The purpose of this workbook is to help you realize why you get those occasional reactions from your listeners, and to take the good English you already have and polish it enough to keep those questions to a bare minimum. And while we're at it, I'd like for you to have some fun.

Who am I, and why did I write this book?

I have been a Speech-Language Pathologist for 37 years. During those years I have worked in public and private schools and universities, hospitals, clinics, homes, and corporate settings. Over the past 12 years I have helped 725 people from more than 40 language backgrounds with their spoken and written English. I prepared this workbook and accompanying CDs in order to help those who do not have access to live classes and tutoring.

Speech-Language Pathologists are trained to analyze the anatomy and physiology of the speech mechanism. We are required to complete a Master's Degree and an internship, and to pass an examination given by a national certification board. The core of what we do is to help people communicate more effectively in a language that they have already learned to speak. I say this so that you will not confuse me with an English teacher. In order for me to help you, you must already be able to have a conversation in English.

This workbook is designed to give you some effective yet fun practice guidelines and drill materials to improve your pronunciation of North American English. It is based on Standard North American pronunciation, the style used by the major news network anchor people. I have aimed for a scientific foundation, but have tried not to be too stuffy or academic. For those who are interested in learning more, I have included a glossary (Appendix C) and a list of resources. Since I want to make this fun, I have avoided use of technical words wherever I could, and opted for the plainest, most straightforward language I could find.

Improving your English pronunciation will take a lot of work, but it shouldn't be boring. I've been telling my clients for years that regardless of their current level of proficiency in English, I have two hopes for them. One is that they move ahead on the proficiency continuum a few notches more, and the other is that they will have fun doing it. That is my wish for you too. One of my favorite professors, Dr. Jay Rosenbek, said that any speech therapist should try to elicit at least one smile per session. I believe that. I also believe that if I haven't done that, I've goofed.

I also love what prolific author, linguist, and philanthropist Suzette Hadin Elgin says in the introduction of her book, The Grandmother Principles, "You can trust me to get you safely to the end of this book." I have tons of experience in leading people through difficulties in the pronunciation of English.

There is no such thing as perfect English.

If you consider spoken English proficiency to fall along a continuum with no English at one end and "perfect " English at the opposite end, you probably fall somewhere in between the halfway mark and the "perfect" end. Your English is already pretty good, or you wouldn't be reading this book. The reason we can say that there is no such thing as perfect English is that even the experts don't always agree about usage and pronunciation. Unlike other languages, English has no governing authority that allows or denies how words are spelled, used, and pronounced. An English dictionary is not a rulebook, but a suggested guideline. It is based on the pronunciation, spelling, and usage of most educated speakers. English is in a constant state of change. For example, "week end" was spelled as two separate words when my mother was a schoolgirl. By the time I was in school, the preferred spelling was "week-end." Somewhere along the line, the preference changed to "weekend," and nobody sent me the memo! So, English is a growing, developing language. As we import more words from other languages, and from increasing technology, we will continue to see changes and variations. Don't be discouraged if you sometimes feel like me, that you didn't get the memo. Even native speakers of English sometimes feel this way.

How this workbook is structured

North American English contains about 44 speech sounds. This workbook is not intended to address all of them. I've only included those that I have found to cause the most grief for people who are speaking English as a second language.

I've divided the workbook so that each section addresses specific problem sounds. Since we have never met, and I have not had the opportunity to evaluate your English pronunciation, please go to **Appendix B-Index of Practice Materials by Language**-and find your mother tongue in the list from the left column. Trace across and note the checkmarks to find the chapters that typically are difficult for ESL (**E**nglish as a **S**econd **L**anguage) speakers of your native language. You may find that some of these no longer apply to you if you are more proficient with English or that you need others if you feel less proficient.

I follow each chapter heading with a brief discussion of the nature of the sound and the difficulty speakers usually have with the sound.

I then list **contrastive pairs.** These are words that compare the desired word with the one the listener will think you have said if your mother tongue causes you to use the contrasted sound. For example, you mean to say that you work in a la**b**, but you don't voice the final /b/. Your listener is going to think you said la**p**, and is going to wonder just what kind of a job you have! Please do not pass over this section. It is essential that you hear these differences before you go on.

When you have spent enough time with the contrastive pairs to hear the differences clearly, you will be ready to go to the **practice words.** Listen to each word and repeat it in the pause provided on the CD. Be sure to record yourself and listen to your practice words. Don't go on until you hear the correct sound. Next, do the **practice sentences** following the same guidelines: listen, repeat, record, and listen for the accuracy of your productions. When you have mastered the sentences, go to the **contrastive pairs in practice sentences** and again follow the same guidelines. After these steps, you will be ready for the tongue twisters, rhymes, and songs at the end of each section.

Notations

You will notice that throughout this workbook, I mark some of the words by their frequency. This is so that you can make some decisions about how to best spend your practice time. For example, the most frequently used word in English is **the.** If you see a word that is ranked as the 187th most frequently used, please don't think, "Gee, how important could number 187 be?" There are 200,000 commonly used words in English. Puts number 187 in a whole new light, doesn't it? I have included the 1,000 most frequently used words in Appendix D.

Words in parentheses behind the first entry in the practice words lists are homophones. For example, in Chapter 2, on initial unvoiced consonants, the 2nd practice word for /t/ is listed as

tail (tale). This tells you that those two words are pronounced exactly alike.

If I use an asterisk (*) after an entry in the contrastive pairs list, it means that this does not exist as a word in English. Such an entry is rather what the word will sound like if the error sound is substituted. I include these entries for you to listen to so that you can compare them with the correct pronunciations of the words.

If I enclose a letter or letters in quotation marks, I mean the spelling. If I enclose in backslashes, I'm referring to the sound. You already know that a spelled letter is not necessarily the sound produced. This is part of the difficulty in pronouncing English. For example, spelled letter "c" may produce a /k/ sound as in "candy" or an /s/ sound as in "city." Please see **Cues for the production of speech sounds" in Appendix A** for tips on pronunciation of individual sounds and for the notations I have used to represent sounds in this workbook. I have used these International Phonetic Alphabet (IPA) symbols as much as I could.

Why Tongue twisters, rhymes, and songs?

Two reasons. The first is that I encourage anything that will make practice more fun. The second is that my clients often ask for them, and I believe they can be the best judges of their own needs. When I first began getting such requests, I was skeptical. After all, nothing in my professional training mentioned any studies or data proving that they help.

Data we do have from neurological studies about the brain and language show that melodic intonation patterns are governed on the opposite side of the brain from speech patterns. That's why some famous singers, despite the fact that they stutter when they speak, can sing with ease and fluency. So maybe there is a physical basis for the hope that melodic types of practice material are more effective. Whether that's true or not, anything that makes practice fun is bound to help, simply because a person who is having fun with the practice is more likely to do the practice.

An important caveat

You must establish the correct sound first. Work through the materials leading up to the tongue twisters and rhymes. Simply reciting the tongue twisters, rhymes, and songs will not help improve the target sound until you first produce the sound correctly. I can promise you one thing. If you do not practice, you will not improve. So let's talk about how you should go about the practice.

Practice considerations

1. Practice for about an hour nearly every day.
2. You'll get better results from practicing for 20 minutes three times a day or 30 minutes twice a day than one time for an hour.
3. On horrifically busy days, know that it is worthwhile to practice for a few minutes while in your car or doing household errands. Don't think that there

is nothing to be gained just because you are too busy to sit at your computer or tape recorder for half an hour. This is why I have included the ***practice on the go*** sections.

4. Always listen closely to the contrastive pairs, and listen for the differences in the sounds before you begin to practice any of the words or sentences.

5. Record yourself! I don't care how high or low tech you are, you must use some means of recording yourself for your own feedback.

6. People nearly always tell me that they can say the troublesome sound just fine when they are thinking about it, but forget to use it during the flow of conversation. This tells me they are doing fine so far, but just need more practice. Focused practice helps. Make note of a couple of words you use often but forget to use correctly. Give them the ***practice on the go*** treatment. Write them on index cards, keep the cards handy, and practice them several times throughout the day.

7. People also tell me that they can say the sound by itself or in words, but not in complete sentences. Again, so far, so good. Just cut the sentences down to short phrases. For example, practice sentence #4 for the short i sound is, "If you're sick of chicken order fish." Suppose you've been practicing the word list and your recording tells you you're sounding terrific, but this sentence causes you to lose control of all those "short i" sounds. Don't worry, just practice the phrase "order fish." When you are comfortable with that much, try, "…sick of chicken…" and so on until you've got the whole sentence.

Let's talk about equipment

In the last century, when I was a speech therapist in training, we used a high tech piece of equipment called a shoebox. I'm serious. You use the empty box that your shoes came in. Hold it to your ear as though it were the receiver on a telephone. Speak into one end and listen to your voice as the box channels the sound to your ear. This will help you hear your voice more critically.

Of course, the equipment of choice in those days was a tape recorder, and I have been using my good old portable until quite recently. I can always tell when it's time for me to bump my technology up to the next level, when my client walks into the room and looks at the device I am using with a mixture of pity and horror. Over the past few years, it has been my clients who have advised me on the latest and greatest recording devices.

For anyone who has a computer, I recommend that you go to the nearest electronics store and get a headset that plugs into a port. I checked recently, and while some headsets are now priced near $100, there are still perfectly adequate ones in the $10 to $15 range. Now, go to the Sound Recorder on your computer. You see that it looks like the buttons on a tape recorder. For convenience, I put mine on my desktop. Click the record button and record yourself practicing a few words or sentences at a time. Then stop and click the play button. The sound quality is marvelous. Of course, by now, many people are using digital recorders that are about the size of a candy bar and can be used anywhere. You have to use the earphones to adequately analyze your voice, and even better, when you get back to your computer, plug it in and listen to your voice for maximum clarity.

Well, whether you use the most recent high tech recording device, your empty shoebox, or some technology in between, it is essential that you listen to yourself-- and often-- for self-analysis.

Ready to start?

Finally, I know that some people will be able to use this workbook and CD to improve their spoken English as a course of independent study. I also know that many will have questions, and some may even like personal assistance. You can always go to my website www.accent-professional.com and use the Request for Information button to send me your questions and requests. I promise a prompt reply.

Now, good luck and have fun!

Part I--Consonants

Introduction to Consonants

A consonant is a speech sound produced by contractions of the speech organs. These include the jaw, lips, tongue, and palate. The movement of these organs causes pressure to modify the breath stream and shape it into different sounds. Some of the resulting sounds are accompanied by vibration of the larynx, or voicing. Others are not. Hence, we have voiced consonants: /b/, /d/, /g/, /v/, /ð/, /z/, /ʒ/, /dʒ/, /m/, /n/, and /ŋ/and unvoiced consonants: /p/, /t/, /k/, /f/, /ɵ/, /s/, /ʃ/ and /tʃ/. (See Appendix A).

It's better to start your pronunciation practice with consonants, because they can be more easily demonstrated and observed.

In addition to whether or not consonants are voiced, they are classified by the manner in which they are produced. So /p, b, t, d, k, g / are stops, sometimes called plosives, because to produce them, you must build up a little air in your mouth and release it suddenly into a puff. Put your hand in front of your mouth and say /p/. Do you feel the puff of air?

Frictions are /f, v, ɵ, ð, s, z, ʃ, ʒ/, so called because it is necessary to create friction by rubbing the air stream through your speech organs. For example, can you feel the friction as you rub a stream of air between your upper teeth and lower lip for a /v/?

The sounds of /tʃ, dʒ/ are called affricates and are simply combinations of the stops /t, d/ with the frictions /ʃ, ʒ/.

The glides /w, j/ are so called because it is necessary to glide from one position with your speech organs to another in order to produce these.

The glottal /h/ is produced by pushing air forcefully through your open vocal cords.

The /l/ and /r/ are classified as semi-vowels because they have some characteristics of both vowels and consonants.

Chapter 1
Final Voiced Consonants

What is voicing?

Whether or not an English sound has voicing (vocal cord vibration), can be critical to what your listener thinks you have said. To know what I mean when I say voiced and unvoiced, place your fingertips lightly on your throat right over your voice box and alternately say /p/, /b/. Don't say, pea, bee; or puh, buh. Make only the sound for the consonant, without any vowel sound after it. Now do the same for /t/, /d/, and for /k/, /g/. You should feel vibration for /b/, /d/, and /g/, but no vibration for /p/, /t/, and /k/.

Pronunciation tip

For this group of sounds, you must take care to voice the sound at the end of the word. If you don't, and you intend to say, "I need a ca**b**", your listener will hear, "I need a ca**p**." If someone asks you, "Where is your book?" and you intend to say, "It's in the ba**g**," your listener will hear, "It's in the ba**ck**." Now your listener wonders. Is your book in the back of your car? Your bookcase? Your sofa? A German friend of mine told me that he would never forget the look on the waiter's face the first time he tried to order crab in an American restaurant! If, when you record your practice of this section, you have difficulty achieving the voiced sound at the end, then try holding the vowel sound before it a bit longer. All vowels are voiced, so this should help carry the voicing through to the end.

Usual spellings

In general, this group behaves very nicely! A "b" spelling gives a /b/ sound, a "d" spelling gives a /d/ sound, and a "g" spelling gives a /g/ sound. An exception is that "mb" endings have silent "b." Examples are lamb, comb, limb, numb, bomb, tomb, and climb.

Contrastive pairs

Voiced /b,d,g/	Unvoiced /p,t,k/
rib	rip
cab	cap
lab	lap
mob	mop
gab	gap
bad	bat
ballad	ballot
fad	fat
hide	height
ride	right (write)
had	hat
need	neat
tag	tack
lag	lack
wig	wick
bug	buck
pig	pick

/b/		/d/		/g/	
1.	crib	10.	bed	19.	beg
2.	tub	11.	did	20.	bug
3.	cab	12.	read	21.	fog
4.	rib	13.	had	22.	leg
5.	knob	14.	ride	23.	pig
6.	bribe	15.	need	24.	dig
7.	robe	16.	hide	25.	drug
8.	tube	17.	made	26.	flag
9.	job	18.	head	27.	dog

Practice sentences

1. I ma**d**e a fla**g** for the party.
2. How much di**d** the ro**b**e cost?
3. I ha**d** a sore le**g** after the race.
4. She coul**d** har**d**ly see the ca**b** in the fo**g**.

5. There's a bu**g** in the baby's cri**b**.
6. I broke my ri**b** and nee**d** a ri**d**e.
7. Why di**d** he hi**d**e the ro**b**e?
8. Here's a be**d** for your do**g**.
9. A pi**g** can di**g** a hole.
10. Rea**d** the warning on the tu**b**e.

Contrastive pairs in practice sentences

1. He left his ca**p** in the ca**b**.
2. The ha**t** ha**d** a red band.
3. Pi**ck** the cutest pi**g** for the fair.
4. I nee**d** a nea**t** work area.
5. Just ta**ck** the ta**g** to the shirt.
6. The bri**d**e wore a brigh**t** smile.
7. A low fa**t** diet is no fa**d**.
8. You can't bring that pu**p** in this pu**b**!
9. It must have been a ba**d** ba**t** that caused him to strike out.
10. He's a smart ki**d** to pack a safety ki**t**.

Tongue Twister Rhyme:

A tree toa**d** love**d** a she-toa**d**
Who live**d** up in a tree.
He was a two-toe**d** tree toa**d**
But a three-toe**d** toa**d** was she.

Fre**d** fe**d** Te**d** brea**d**, and Te**d** fe**d** Fre**d** brea**d**. (This one is also great for the /ɛ/--see Chapter 19).

Practice on the go!!

The fourth most frequently used word in the English language is "an**d**." As you go about your daily tasks, say aloud, "I'll use salt an**d** pepper." "I'll invite John an**d** Mary." "I need eggs an**d** butter." The 28ᵗʰ most frequently used word is "ha**d**." Again, think about your daily activities and say, " I ha**d** everything I nee**d**e**d**." "She ha**d** her work done by noon." "We ha**d** a great time."

A special note: When to finish a past tense word with /t/, and when with /d/

Have you ever noticed that some past tense endings, while spelled with "ed", are pronounced as /t/? Will you be comforted to know that there is an ironclad rule for knowing when to pronounce /t/ at the end of a regular past verb? Here it is:

If the final sound of a regular verb is not voiced, then don't voice the –ed ending.
Examples are backed (backt), picked (pickt), hoped (hopt), capped (capt), leafed

(leaft), passed (past), mashed (masht), and hatched (hatcht). And no, you must not pronounce an additional syllable for these endings either.

You do pronounce an additional syllable when the final letter is already a "t" or a "d", like these: waited (wait əhd), dated (dat əhd), traded (trad əhd), and faded (fad əhd).
Here's the astounding thing about this rule. It has no exceptions. We can't say that about English very often.

Chapter 2
Initial Unvoiced Consonants

What are unvoiced sounds?

To know what I mean when I say unvoiced, rest your fingertips lightly on your larynx (voice box) and alternately say /p/, /b/. Don't say, pea, bee; or puh, buh. Make only the sound for the consonant alone, without any vowel sound after it. Now do the same for /t/, /d/, and for /k/, /g/. You should feel vibration for /b/, /d/, and /g/, but no vibration for /p/, /t/, and /k/. This is the difference between voiced and unvoiced sounds, and that difference is mighty important!
When I speak of voiced and unvoiced in my classes people will often think that by unvoiced, I mean no sound. This is not the case. Unvoiced sounds are like whispers. You can certainly hear them. It's just that your vocal cords are not in vibration for unvoiced sounds.
For this group, you must take care not to voice initial consonants /p/, /t/, and /k/, lest they sound like their voiced counterparts /b/, /d/, and /g/. Here's what can happen. You ask, "Is it **p**acked?" And your listener, looking very puzzled, asks, "**B**acked by what?" In the restaurant, you say, "I'd like **p**ie." And the waiter asks, "What would you like to **b**uy?" Have you ever meant to say "time" and your listener heard "dime," or meant to say, "came" and your listener heard "game"? This section is for you!

Pronunciation tip

Try using a bigger puff of air after the /p/, /t/, or /k/ sound.

Spelling tips

As for the voiced final consonants in Chapter 1, these usually behave in a regular fashion. That is, a "p" spelling should give a /p/ sound and "t" spelling should give a /t/ sound. The notable irregularity about the "k" sound is that it is sometimes spelled with the letter "c" as in candy and coffee.

Contrastive pairs

Unvoiced /p,t,k/	Voiced /b,d,g/
peach	beach
pit	bit
pill	bill
peas	bees
tin	din
tip	dip
time	dime
town	down
coal	goal
cane	gain
cold	gold
could	good

Practice words (Practice tip: a bigger puff of air with these can work wonders!)

	/p/		/t/		/k/
1.	pack	1.	tame	1.	cake
2.	pad	2.	tail (tale)	2.	call
3.	palm	3.	ten	3.	cat
4.	park	4.	time	4.	key
5.	pat	5.	took	5.	keep
6.	patch	6.	tooth	6.	come
7.	pet	7.	toy	7.	could
8.	pig	8.	tax	8.	cold
9.	pony	9.	tin	9.	coat
10.	pin	10.	tip	10.	coffee
11.	pole	11.	test	11.	card
12.	pear	12.	top	12.	code

Practice sentences

1. **P**ack the **c**ake **c**arefully.
2. There are **t**en **c**ats at the shelter.
3. He **p**ut the **k**eys in my **p**alm.

4. **P**at took the **p**ony **t**o the **p**asture.
5. **K**eep the **p**ears in the **c**ooler.
6. Don't throw your **p**each **p**its out the window!
7. **C**ome **t**o the **p**ark for a **p**icnic.
8. She bought him a **t**oy **p**ig.
9. The **t**ax **c**ode is **c**onfusing.
10. Do you have **t**ime **t**o help me **p**ack?

Contrastive pairs in practice sentences

1. **C**ould you help us find a **g**ood book?
2. The **b**ill for the **p**ills was outrageous.
3. We ate **p**each pie at the **b**each.
4. **B**ees attacked us while we were shelling **p**eas.
5. Let's go **d**owntown.
6. The **g**oat ate my **c**oat!
7. There was a **g**ain in the sugar **c**ane market.
8. **D**ip the **t**ip of the cookie in chocolate

Two old rhymes

Peter, **P**eter, **p**umpkin eater,
Had a wife and **c**ouldn't **k**eep her,
He **p**ut her in a **p**umpkin shell;
And there he **k**ept her very well.
--Mother Goose

Tick, **t**ock, **t**ick, **t**ock,
Merrily sings the **cl**ock;
It's **t**ime for work,
It's **t**ime for play,
So it sings throughout the day.

Tongue twister

The **two-twenty-two train t**ore through the **t**unnel.

Practice on the go!!

The word "to" is the third most frequently used word in the English language. Practicing it has the added benefit of carry-over to its homophones, "too" and "two", also used with high frequency. Therefore, take advantage of every spare moment throughout the day: walking to a meeting, driving from here to there, or waiting for your children, your spouse, your dog, and say, "Go **to** _____ "(the store, a movie, work, class, etc.).

Chapter 3
Two Special /t/ Sounds

Have you ever noticed that in British English, middle t's are produced with a more pronounced puff of air than in American English? When we say, "letter," "butter," and "water," we make them sound close to a /d/. Speech therapists will sometimes refer to these as "flap t's."

There is another special case when a "t" spelling in the weak (unstressed) syllable of a word is followed by an "n." Samples of this can be heard in the words "button," "cotton," "mountain," and "fountain." In these, the vowel between the "t" and the "n" is replaced by a glottal catch. That's just a speech therapist's way of naming what happens in your throat when you say, "uh-oh."

If you do not adopt these two special sounds of North American English, you will still be understood. They are not as important as the other sounds in this book from the standpoint that lack of their use will not cause your meaning to be mistaken. They are, however, important if you want your English to sound smoother and more native. As Professor Lorna Sikorski says, they are part of the "insider trader secrets to speaking English like a native."

Practice words for flap t

1. better
2. letter
3. pretty
4. wanted
5. water
6. butter
7. later
8. lettuce
9. pity
10. total
11. biting
12. putting
13. pouting
14. putter
15. bitter
16. party
17. metal
18. bottle

Practice words for glottal t

1. button
2. curtain
3. certain
4. flatten
5. kitten
6. mitten
7. rotten
8. cotton
9. Dayton
10. Manhattan
11. mountain
12. eaten
13. sweeten
14. satin
15. forgotten
16. Latin
17. botany
18. remittance
19. accountant

Practice sentences for flap t

1. She's setting the table with pretty water glasses.
2. The pouting putter missed his putt.
3. We need forty bottles of wine for the reception.
4. The rabbits have been eating my lettuce.
5. I'd better write a letter.
6. It's a pity the party was rained out.
7. What makes this water taste so bitter?
8. The total we wanted was higher.
9. The thermos bottle is metal.
10. Put the butter away later.

Good luck with this tongue twister!

Betty Botter had some butter,
"But," she said, "this butter's bitter.
If I bake this bitter butter,
it would make my batter bitter.
But a bit of better butter--
that would make my batter better."

So she bought a bit of butter,
better than her bitter butter,
and she baked it in her batter,
and the batter was not bitter.
So 'twas better Betty Botter
bought a bit of better butter.

It made the bitter batter better! After you've mastered the flap t's in the Betty Botter passage, remember it to practice again for the vowel changes after you've mastered those.(Chapters 15-22).

Practice sentences for glottal t

1. I ordered the curtains from Dayton.
2. The remittance for the buttons is enclosed.
3. They met in botany class.
4. Have you forgotten to sweeten the tea?
5. She lost her mitten on the mountain.
6. Our accountant wore a satin blouse.
7. We prefer cotton in summer.
8. We went to Manhattan last week.
9. Have you eaten?
10. The apples were rotten.

Song for practicing glottal t

She'll be comin' round the mountain when she comes.
She'll be comin' round the mountain when she comes.
She'll be comin' round the mountain,
She'll be comin' round the mountain,
She'll be comin' round the mountain when she comes.

Practice on the go!!

The 90th most frequently used word is "water." The 113th is "little. These are both flap t's.

The 131st most frequently used word is "sentence." The 288th is "mountain." These are both glottal t's.

"The garden needs a little water." "I need a little water." "She needs a little water." "He needs a little water."

Replace she and he with names of family and friends.

Chapter 4
/v/ and /w/

ESL speakers such as Korean and Spanish sometimes get their /v/ and /b/ switched. Did you wear your **v**est, or your **b**est? Well, maybe it was your best vest! German and Indian speakers sometimes get tangled up between /v/ and /w/. Be **v**ery **w**ary of this!

Pronunciation tip

A /v/ sound is a labiodental fricative. In plain English, bite your bottom lip and hum. For the /b/ sound, you must put your lips together, and release the air stream abruptly in a little explosion of sound while humming. So we see two ways that /v/ and /b/ are different: 1. It's lips against teeth for /v/ and lips together for /b/. 2. The breath stream and humming are continuous for /v/, but abrupt for /b/. I promise you that you will never need the /b/ sound for a "v" spelling in English. I also promise that you will never need the /v/ sound for a "b" spelling in English.

If you need a /w/ sound, you pucker your lips as if to whistle and glide them into a smile without letting them touch your teeth. You will never need a /w/ sound for a "v" spelling in English, nor will you ever need a /v/ sound for a "w" spelling in English. Be careful not to let your lips rub your front teeth while making a /w/, or it may sound like a /v/.

Spelling tip

The sound of /v/ is spelled with the letter "v" and the sound of /b/ is spelled with the letter "b." Convenient for a change, right? English pronunciation is not always so logical. Occasionally the spelled letter "o" gives a /w/ pronunciation, as in **o**nce and **o**ne.

Contrastive pairs

/v/	/b/	/w/
very	berry	wary
vase	base	
vat	bat	
vine		wine
vest	best	west
vent	bent	went
veal	we'll	
rove	robe	
curve	curb	
suave	swab	

Practice words for /v/

1. visit
2. value
3. vase
4. vault
5. view
6. vote
7. voice
8. vine
9. vest
10. clover
11. cover
12. envelope
13. driver
14. every
15. never
16. over
17. seven
18. rival
19. above
20. believe
21. five
22. glove
23. give
24. live
25. love
26. sleeve
27. stove

Practice sentences for /v/

1. Who will you **v**isit on your **v**acation?
2. There are se**v**en en**v**elopes in the glo**v**e box.
3. This is a **v**aluable **v**ase.
4. We heard his **v**oice abo**v**e us.
5. Put on glo**v**es before you pull those **v**ines.
6. A **v**est has no slee**v**es.
7. The ri**v**al bank has a new **v**ault.
8. I belie**v**e she ne**v**er got o**v**er it.
9. You'll lo**v**e the ocean **v**iew!
10. E**v**ery dri**v**er belie**v**es in the **v**alue of safety.

Practice words for /w/

1. walk	10. will	19. work
2. want	11. wash	20. would
3. was	12. wax	21. always
4. water	13. weed	22. awake
5. way	14. wind	23. backward
6. we	15. wish	24. between
7. well	16. with	25. everyone
8. went	17. won	26. unwind
9. were	18. word	27. sandwich

Practice sentences for /w/

1. **W**illie is **w**ashing the **w**indows and **w**alls.
2. I **w**ish **W**ilma **w**ould **w**ake up.
3. Don't **w**alk in the **w**oods **wh**ile they are **w**et.
4. Every**o**ne **w**ill **w**ant a sand**w**ich.
5. **W**e are going **w**est this **w**inter.
6. **W**e **w**ish he **w**ould **w**atch his **w**ords.
7. **W**ishing for **w**ealth is **o**ne **w**ay to **w**aste time un**w**isely.

Contrastive pairs in practice sentences

/v/ vs. /b/

1. These are **v**ery good **b**erries.
2. The cur**v**e in that sidewalk makes it tricky to park at the cur**b**.
3. There's a wooden **b**ase for the **v**ase.
4. Don't ro**v**e around in your ro**b**e.
5. A **b**at flew into the **v**at.
6. It isn't sua**v**e to swa**b** your ears in public!

/v/ vs. /w/

7. It's popular to wear a **v**est out **W**est.
8. She **w**ent to check on the **v**ent.
9. **W**e'll have **v**eal for dinner.
10. Tend the grape**v**ines if you expect to have **w**ine.

Tongue Twister for /v/

Vincent vowed vengeance very vehemently.

And an old rhyme

As I Was Going to St. Ives

As I was going to St. Ives,
I met a man with seven wives,
Each wife had seven sacks,
Each sack had seven cats,
Each cat had seven kits,
Kits, cats, sacks, and wives,
How many were going to St. Ives?

Tongue twister for /w/

Who washed Washington's white woolen underwear
when Washington's washerwoman went west?

Practice on the go!!

For /v/

The word "have" is the 24th most frequently used in English. Throughout the day, tell yourself:
I have enough time. I have work to do. I have the book. I have some reading to do. I have to
stop at the store. I have never met him……………………..

And the practice is perhaps even more effective if you use the contraction, I've. It's the same
sound, and it is, after all, the way we speak.

For /w/

The 12th most frequently used word in English is "was". Try these:

1. It was nice yesterday.
2. He was at work.
3. I was ready early.
4. She was my best friend.
5. It was a good meal.
6. It was kind of you.
7. He was out west.
8. It was tricky.
9. It was raining.
10. It was a long time ago.
11. It was a beautiful spring.
12. It was a nice party.

13. The sun was shining.
14. The wind was blowing.
15. The snow was falling.
16. It was a hot day.
17. He was a doctor.
18. She was a scientist.
19. He was winning.
20. She was finished

Make up your own!!

Chapter 5
Unvoiced "th" /θ/

European Spanish is, I understand, the only language besides English that uses this sound. That may be why it presents difficulties for most other ESL speakers.

Pronunciation tip

The tongue-tip is slightly between the front teeth and riding on a gentle breath stream. There is a very small margin of distance between a /s/ and a /θ/. If you pull your tongue tip back even slightly from between your teeth, you will produce a /s/ instead of a /θ/ and your listener will think you have said sink, or pass instead of path. This is a common problem for many ESL speakers, particularly Asians and Germans.

For Middle-Eastern, Nigerian, and Indian ESL speakers, make sure that the breath stream is constant and the tongue to teeth contact is gentle, or your listener is going to hear fate when you meant to say faith, and tree when you meant to say three.

For other ESL speakers, including French, make sure to keep your upper teeth away from your lower lip, or your listener will hear fought when you meant to say thought, and deaf when you meant to say death.

Contrastive pairs

/θ/	/s/	/θ/	/t/	/θ/	/f/
thin	sin	thin	tin	thin	fin
thing	sing	thigh	tie	three	free
think	sink	thick	tick	thought	fought
math	mass	math	mat	wreath	reef
truth	truce	bath	bat	sheath	sheaf
bath	bass	faith	fate	death	deaf

Practice word lists

1. thank	10. theater	19. mouth	28. author
2. thaw	11. through	20. north	29. healthy
3. theft	12. thought	21. south	30. nothing
4. third	13. thigh	22. path	31. faithful
5. three	14. bath	23. teeth	32. birthday
6. thousand	15 both	24. with	33. bathtub
7. thin	16. cloth	25. breath	34. truthful
8. thick	17. fourth	26. faith	35. anything
9. theory	18. month	27. youth	36. ethical

Practice sentences

1. It's his four**th** bir**th**day.
2. They need **th**ree yards of clo**th**.
3. Odd-numbered highways run nor**th** and sou**th**.
4. She's always tru**th**ful about every**th**ing.
5. This is the au**th**or's **th**irteen**th** book.
6. We bo**th** went to the **th**eater.
7. He **th**inks my **th**eory is pa**th**etic.
8. Jim's office is on the twelf**th** floor.
9. There are **th**irty-**th**ree cars in the race.
10. I **th**ought I could **th**aw my frozen fingers wi**th** my brea**th**.

Contrastive pairs in practice sentences.

1. She did her ma**th** after Ma**ss**.
2. I **th**ink a paper boat will **s**ink.
3. He's so hoarse he can't **s**ing a **th**ing!
4. A sheet of **t**in is **th**in.
5. **Th**anks for the **f**ree **t**anks of gas!
6. Leave your ma**th** assignment under my doorma**t**.
7. His fai**th** will decide his fate.

8. There are **th**ree **f**ree samples left.
9. I **th**ought they **f**ought hard.
10. We placed a wrea**th** at the ree**f**.

Tongue twister

Thirty **th**ousand **th**oughtless boys
Thought they'd make a **th**undering noise.
So with **th**irty **th**ousand **th**umbs,
They **th**umped on **th**irty **th**ousand drums.

Practice on the go!!

Think about your day and say, "I **th**ink _____." (I got a lot done, she was a big help, I'll have chicken for dinner, I got a good deal, the presentation went well…etc.)
Be sure to repeat, "I **th**ink…" each time.

Chapter 6
Voiced "th" /ð/

There are not huge numbers of words with this sound. The problem is that 11 of them are in the top 100 most frequently used words in English. At least one of them will occur in nearly every sentence you speak. **See Appendix D for the 1,000 most frequent words.**

Pronunciation tip

To produce this sound, place just the very tip of your tongue between your front teeth, use some friction, blow and hum. It's like the /ɵ/ (voiceless th) in the previous section, but you add voice.

Spelling tip

In nearly every class I've ever conducted, people have expressed surprise that the "th" in "clothes" is silent. This word is pronounced exactly like "close."

Voiced th contrastive pairs

/ð/ (initials)	/d/	/ð/ (finals)	/d/	/ð/	/z/
than	Dan	breathe	breed	thee	Z
then	den	loathe	load	then	Zen
they	day	teethe	teed	breathe	breeze
there	dare	seethe	seed		

Practice words

1. the	10. another	19. bathe
2. than	11. bother	20. clothe
3. their(there)	12. other	21. smooth
4. that	13. father	22. breathe
5. them	14. mother	
6. this	15. although	
7. these	16. either	
8. though	17. weather (whether)	
9. they	18. brother	

Practice sentences

1. It's hard to brea**the** in this wea**the**r.
2. **Th**at hat has a red fea**the**r.
3. **Th**ey are my mo**the**r and fa**the**r.
4. Birds of a fea**the**r flock toge**the**r.
5. **Th**ey gathered all her bro**the**rs toge**the**r.
6. **Th**ey don't bo**the**r to ba**the** every day.
7. **Th**e smoo**th** lea**the**r jacket is mine.
8. We'll go, whe**the**r or not the wea**the**r cooperates.

Contrastive pairs in practice sentences

1. **Th**ey had a nice **d**ay.
2. I **d**are you to go **th**ere.
3. She'd rather go with **D**an **th**an Bill.
4. Wash the glasses, and **th**en put them in the **d**en.
5. I'm going to **d**oze if you read **th**ose!
6. I love to brea**the** a spring bree**z**e.

A rhyme for practicing /ð/

The Bow That Has No Arrow
Which is **th**e bow **th**at has no arrow?
The rainbow **th**at never killed a sparrow.
Which is **th**e singer **th**at has but one song?
The cuckoo, who sings it all day long.

"The" practice: The most frequently used word in the English language is "the".

1. The garden looks nice in the spring.
2. The pliers go in the toolbox.
3. The orange blossom is the state flower of Florida.
4. The pearl is the birthstone for June.
5. The tulip poplar is the state tree for Indiana.
6. The dog is chasing the squirrel.
7. The cardinal is the state bird for Indiana.
8. The pie is in the oven.
9. The lark is on the wing.
10. The children are on the bus.
11. The cat is chasing the mouse.
12. The sun is in the sky.
13. The plate is on the table.
14. The speaker is at the podium.
15. The bank is on the corner.
16. The car is in the driveway.
17. The books are in the car.
18. The milk is in the refrigerator.
19. The baby is in the crib.
20. The cook is in the kitchen.

Practice on the go!!

You get the idea. Now make up your own sentences like those above!

Bonus practice (The 25th most frequent word in English is "this." See Chapter 15 for that troublesome /ɪ/ in this and **is**).

Read each sentence aloud.
1. This is my son.
2. This is my book.
3. This weather is beautiful.
4. This is my home.
5. What is this?
6. This coffee is too strong.
7. This house needs painting.
8. What did you do this afternoon.
9. Is this your daughter?
10. I like this coat.
11. This is a nice place.
12. Is this clock right?
13. This is my office.

14. Is this your desk?
15. Is this the right place?
16. How do you like this hat?
17. This is my wife.
18. This is a beautiful painting.
19. Is this your newspaper?
20. This is not what I ordered.
21. This room is too cold.
22. What are you doing this weekend?
23. Was this for you?
24. He is coming over this weekend.
25. What is the name of this song

Chapter 7
Nasal consonant /ŋ/

There are only three sounds of English that are supposed to resonate in the nose: /m/, /n/, and /ŋ/.

The two usual things to go wrong with the /ŋ/ sound are:

1. Some front it to the /n/ position. (Ah hah! Did you know "front" could be a verb?)
2. Some give a /g/ or "hard g" sound after the /ŋ/.

In the first case, the word si**ng** will sound like si**n**. In the second case, it will sound like "singuh," which is not a word in English. The frequency of use of this sound comes primarily from the -ing endings of verbs and gerunds. Do you remember gerunds? They look like verbs but function as nouns in your sentence. For example, "Swimming is strenuous." "The running of the third race will begin at 3 o'clock."

Pronunciation tip

The rule is that all words ending in –ng are pronounced with the back of the tongue in the /g/ position, (see **Appendix A—Cues for the production of speech sounds**) but held in place and hummed through the nose. In other words, pretend you are about to make a /g/, but don't release it. If a suffix is added, the /ŋ/ sound remains the same. An example is si**ng**, si**ng**er, si**ng**ing.

Contrastive pairs

/ŋ/	/n/	/ŋg/
wing	win	winguh*
bang	ban	banguh*
rang	ran	ranguh*
tongue	ton	tonguh*
fang	fan	fanguh*
guarding	garden	guardinguh*

Practice tips

1. If your difficulty is in producing the /ŋ/ in the back of your mouth, and instead you bring your tongue to the front where it will sound like an /n/, all you have to do is realize that the proper position for /ŋ/ is the same as for /k/ and /g/. From the /k, g/ position, instead of releasing the tongue, just hold it there and hum through your nose.
2. If the trouble is that you are sounding like /ŋg/ instead of /ŋ/, you are already in the correct position, but you should simply leave the back of your tongue in place and not release it.

Practice words

1. bring	10. asking	19. hanger (hangar)
2. king	11. coming	20. kingdom
3. long	12. doing	21. singer
4. lung	13. going	22. strongly
5. ring	14. making	23. ringer (wringer)
6. sing	15. morning	24. flinging
7. spring	16. playing	25. longing
8. wrong	17. working	26. gingham
9. tongue	18. writing	27. gangster

Practice sentences

1. Bring the king a golden ring.
2. We wear gingham in the spring.
3. The singer has been working all morning.
4. Her lungs are going strong!
5. The gangster is hiding in the hangar.
6. If your tongue is in the wrong spot you may be trying too hard.
7. She's flinging the hangers all over the bedroom.
8. We've been longing for spring.

9. She's been writi**ng** all day lo**ng**.
10. I stro**ng**ly advise you to keep worki**ng**.

Contrastive pairs in practice sentences

1. He's going to wi**n** with his wi**ng** design.
2. It's no si**n** to si**ng** in the spri**ng**.
3. They ra**n** when the bell ra**ng**.
4. After all this practice, my to**ng**ue weighs a to**n**.
5. The snake caught its fa**ng** in the fa**n**.
6. Did you hear a ba**ng**? I thought there was a ba**n** on firecrackers!
7. My dog is guardi**ng** the garde**n** from rabbits.
8. The knitter wove ribbo**n** into the ribbi**ng**.
9. What would have kept this rotte**n** wood from rotti**ng**?
10. Has she been baki**ng** with baco**n**?

Practice Rhymes

Sing a song all day long
It can't be wrong to sing a song.

When I go fishing
I'm always wishing
Some fishes I will get
But while I'm fishing
The fish are wishing
I won't; just harder yet.

Practice on the go!!

Think of the things you or someone else could bring to a picnic at the beach. Bri**ng** a towel. Bri**ng** some salad. _____sunscreen. _____pickles, fruit, cheese, deviled eggs, a big umbrella, etc.

A few exceptions: What? English pronunciation has exceptions??

Pronounce longer, longest, stronger, strongest, younger, and youngest with an additional "hard g" after the /ŋ/, (long-ger, long-gest, etc.). As with other languages, some words just will not conform to the rules.

Here's another trick. If a word has an -ng spelling in the middle, and you take off the letters after the -ng, and you are not left with a whole word at all, pronounce the -ng with a hard g after it as above. Examples are finger (fing-ger), anger (ang-ger), and language (lang-guage). Notice in the further examples that follow, if you take the letters after the ng away from the word, and you are left without a real word, or you do have a real word such as "sing" but it has a completely different meaning, (singly means one at a time, not to make music with your voice), then you should pronounce a hard g after the /ŋ/.

More examples:

angler	angrily	bangle	languor	mangle
singly	mongrel	tangle	jingle	hunger

Chapter 8
Consonant /z/

ESL speakers whose first language is Spanish are already doing this sound just fine, but without the necessary humming, or voicing, which converts the /s/ sound to a /z/. If you asked about the prize, and your listener thought you said price, this is your section.

Pronunciation tip

Place your tongue behind your upper teeth just at the gum line. Close your teeth lightly and blow down the center of the tongue while humming. In other words, just do what you've been doing for /s/, but add voice.

Spelling tip

This sound is usually spelled with a "z", but be aware that it often is spelled with an "s." Don't you love English? Such a logical language! I'll talk more about that at the end of this section.

Contrastive pairs

/z/	/s/		/z/	/s/
zeal	seal		buzz	bus
zip	sip		prize	price
zinc	sink (sync)		flees (fleas)	fleece
zoo	sue (Sue)		graze (grays)	grace
lose	loose		eyes	ice

Practice words

1. zeal	10. eyes	19. nose	28. crazy
2. zebra	11. his	20. rise	29. daisy
3. zero	12. please	21. size	30. dozen
4. zest	13. surprise	22. tease	31. easy
5. zinc	14. these	23. use (verb)	32. music
6. zone	15. those	24. was	33. deserve
7. zoo	16. choose	25. busy	34. disaster
8. as	17. always	26. closet	35. pleasant
9. because	18. lose	27. cousin	36. hazard

Practice sentences

1. I always choose a pleasant surprise for her birthday.
2. The crazy zebra zipped through the zoo.
3. My cousin's closet is a disaster zone.
4. We're always pleased to see you.
5. You deserve a dozen roses.
6. Please don't tease me about my nose.
7. Her eyes show her zeal for the music.
8. It isn't easy to choose the right size.
9. How many zeros are in your zip code?
10. You take these and I'll take those.

Contrastive pairs in practice sentences

1. Sue has gone to the zoo.
2. Choose the seal with zeal.
3. Sip your coffee before you zip to work.
4. They installed a zinc sink in their kitchen.
5. My pearls are so loose (s) I'm afraid I'll lose (z) them.
6. Find a prize at a lower price.
7. Oops! There are fleas in this fleece.
8. Do the antelope graze with grace?
9. She heard the buzz on the bus.
10. Put ice on your eyes to reduce the swelling.

Thousand most frequently used words: /s/ and /z/ endings:

I've extracted the following from the 1000 most frequently used words in English. The numbers are the word's frequency of use. The words in the left column, those pronounced /z/ although spelled "s" are not so many, and are well worth memorizing since their frequency of use is so high. I'll discuss the rules that explain why an "s" spelling can pronounce as /z/ at the end of this section. For most of this list, however, there doesn't seem to be a good explanation.

/z/	**/s/**
7. is	25. this
12. was	
17. as	
19. his	
44. use (verb)	use (noun)
66. these	
74. has	107. place
140. cause	131. sentence
151. does	
187. house (verb)	house (noun)
	190. us
	229. cross
	244. press
245. close (verb, noun)	close (adjective, adverb)
261. ease	
264. always	
266. those	281. science
	290. once
	291. base
	292. horse
	298. face
320. pose	329. class
	342. piece ("peace" is a homophone)
	345. pass
	346. since
	350. space
	374. less
	399. notice
	400. voice
	448. produce
	454. course
	458. force
	462. surface
	488. miss
	494. yes
517. size	510. dance
	523. ice
	531. perhaps
	554. race
563. exercise	577. glass
	578. grass

/z/	/s/
	588. gas
607. raise	
634. phrase	650. sense
	652. else
	655. case
	677. dress
679. surprise	698. crease
	703. office
723. rise	
741. choose	754. practice
758. please	
761. whose	790. thus
	799. process
	800. guess
	820. famous
	855. success
877. noise	879. chance
896. nose	921. discuss
	925. experience
	932. mass
	957. substance

all "ce" and "ss" endings are pronounced /s/

all "x" endings are pronounced /ks/ e.g. box, fix (not included in this list)

If the same word is used as both a verb and a noun, use the /z/ pronunciation for the verb and the /s/ for the noun. See the explanation below in rules for pronunciation of plurals.

Tongue twister for /z/

The la**z**y ja**zz** mu**s**ician jogged to the **z**oo just to view the **z**ebra phy**s**ician.

Note: Spanish ESL speakers can get a lot of mileage from this one since it also exercises your /dʒ/ sound.

Practice on the go!!

The 7th most frequently used word in English is "is", the 12th is "was" the 17th is "as" and the 19th is "his." All of these final "s" spellings pronounce as /z/. Try, "His car is red." "His wife is pretty." "His son is five." "His office is near." "His shirt is new." "His jacket is brown." "His name is Al." How many can you come up with on your own?

Why is "s" sometimes pronounced /z/?

Have you ever noticed that "ice" and "eyes" do not have the same ending sound?

This question comes up in all of my classes. Some people have been taught the rules of plural and possessive /s/ and /z/ pronunciation, and some have not. For those who have not, here is the rule:

> If a noun ends with a voiced sound, e.g. ba**g**, do**g**, tu**b**, ri**b**, be**d**, roa**d**, hi**v**e, ca**v**e, then you must pronounce its plural or possessive ending voiced to match. So it's bags (bagz), dogs (dogz), tubs (tubz), ribs (ribz), beds (bedz), roads (roadz), hives (hivez), and caves (cavez).

> If the noun already ends with a sibilant sound—you know, those hissing, buzzing sounds, then you must pronounce an additional syllable, and still use a /z/ sound. Examples are glasses (glass əz), dishes (dish əz), matches (match əz) and bridges (bridge əz).

Don't forget to apply this rule to names. Who does the book belong to? It's Mary's (Mary'z), Bob's (Bob'z), Joyce's (Joyce'əz), or Dan's (Dan'z).

Since most names and most nouns end voiced, you'll be sounding the /z/ for most of the plurals and possessives you use.

This explains why many "s" spellings are pronounced as a /z/ sound. Here's an explanation for what may seem like another vagary of English pronunciation. For words ending in "se" that are used both as nouns or adjectives and as verbs, pronounce the noun as /s/, and the verb as /z/. Examples: We intend to house (verb=houze) the guests at our house. Close (verb=cloze) the door and sit close to me. What use (noun) will you make of this cloth? I'll use (verb=uze) it to line our booth at the bazaar.

Of course, even these two rules won't explain all the occurrences of "s" spellings pronounced as /z/. I'm afraid there is no good explanation for some. I do hope, however, that this has cleared the matter up a bit for you!

Chapter 9
s-blends

In English, words beginning with the sounds of /sp/ as in spell, /st/ as in stand, /sk/ as in skip, /sm/ as in smile, /sn/ as in snail, /sl/ as in slow, /sw/ as in sweet, /spr/ as in spray, /str/ as in street, and /spl/ as in splash, should start immediately with the /s/ sound. Speakers of Spanish and Farsi will often begin these words with the "eh" vowel in front of the /s/, so that they sound like "espell, estand, eskip." It is important to eliminate this initial vowel sound when speaking these words in English.

Practice tip:

Start these words as though you were making a hissing sound—"sss".

Contrastive pairs (Remember, the items in the second column are not real words.)

/s/	/es/
skin	eskin*
slow	eslow*
smart	esmart*
snow	esnow*
speak	espeak*
stamp	estamp*
swim	eswim*
script	escript*
splash	esplash*
spring	espring*
street	estreet*

More contrastive pairs (The items in the second column here are real words.)

/s/	/ɛs/
spouse	espouse
spy	espy
squire	esquire
state	estate
steam	esteem
strange	estrange

Practice words

1. slow	10. smart	19. spin	28. spray
2. slice	11. smoke	20. stay	29. spread
3. sleep	12. smell	21. stop	30. spring
4. sly	13. sneeze	22. stand	31. splash
5. skate	14. sniff	23. steam	32. split
6. school	15. snow	24. stew	33. strike
7. scold	16. spell	25. sweep	34. straight
8. skim	17. span	26. swim	35. square
9. small	18. speak	27. swell	36. script

Practice sentences

1. Do you **sm**ell **sm**oke?
2. There is too much **sc**olding at that **sch**ool.
3. **St**eam poured off the **st**ew.
4. **St**op at the **st**oplight.
5. I like to hear the rain **spl**ash in the **spr**ing.
6. That **sm**ell made me **sn**eeze.
7. I think it would be **sm**art to **sl**ow down.
8. **Spr**ead jam on a **sl**ice of bread.
9. Will you **st**ay and help me **sw**eep?
10. She read **str**aight from the **scr**ipt.

Contrastive pairs in sentences

1. Will you **esp**ouse the campaign for your **sp**ouse?
2. Use your opera glasses. You might **esp**y a **sp**y.
3. **Squ**ire Anderson has earned the title of **Esqu**ire.
4. What's the **st**ate of his **est**ate?

5. Was the inventor of the **st**eam engine held in **est**eem?
6. It's **str**ange to feel **estr**anged from her.

Tongue twisters

Strict strong stringy Stephen Stretch slickly snared six sickly slinky snakes.

Strange strategic statistics.

Six slippery snails slid slowly seaward.

Practice on the go!!

How many things can you think of to start? **St**art the car. **St**art the process. **St**art the washer. **St**art the day. **St**art the meeting. **St**art the coffee. **St**art walking. **St**art reading.

Chapter 10
Glottal Glide /h/

Some speakers delete this sound. The difficulty is particularly prevalent in those whose first language is French. Did you **h**eat your sandwich or eat your sandwich? Maybe you did both!

Pronunciation tip

Production of this sound is a forceful expulsion of air with no voice, similar to a single heavy pant after running.

Spelling tip

Whenever the letter "h" is spelled at the beginning of a word, you should start the word with this sound. The only exceptions in American English are "heir," "hour," "honest," "honor," "herb," and variants of these such as "heiress," "hourly," and "honorable." For these only, the "h" is silent.

Contrastive pairs

/h/	/ɸ/
heat	eat
hate	ate
hill	ill
hit	it
heel	eel
he's	ease

/h/	/Φ/
hear	ear
hair	air
hire	ire
howl	owl
ham	am
high	I
harm	arm

Practice words

1. had	10. hello	19. how
2. half	11. help	20. who
3. hand	12. hen	21. ahead
4. happy	13. her	22. anyhow
5. has	14. hide	23. behave
6. have	15. high	24. behind
7. he	16. him	25. grasshopper
8. head	17. home	26. perhaps
9. hear	18. horse	27. rehearse

Practice sentences

1. Have you said hello to her?
2. He hid the horse behind the house.
3. Perhaps we can rehearse at home.
4. How high can he jump?
5. He'll be happy to help you.
6. Will you hand me half of that ham?
7. Her doll's head is hollow.
8. I dropped ham salad on my hem.
9. He had a happy childhood.
10. Harry can't get the hang of his horn.
11. The 4-H symbol stands for heart, head, health and hands.

Contrastive pairs in practice sentences

1. Heat and eat foods are convenient.
2. Hit it!
3. Herb has an herb garden. (Remember that "herb" the aromatic plant has a silent "h" but the man's name Herb retains the aspirate /h/.)
4. This may harm your arm.
5. I am fond of ham.
6. The lady on the hill is ill.

7. **H**old this **o**ld vase carefully.
8. An **ee**l bit my **h**eel.
9. The **h**ailstorm made him **ai**l.
10. Her **ey**es said, "**hi**".
11. **A**ll of us stood in the **h**all.
12. The **ai**r lifted her **h**air.
13. She **h**ad an **a**d agency.
14. He **h**as **a**s much as he wants.
15. I **h**ear well with my left **ea**r.
16. **I'**d better **h**ide.
17. **I** feel **h**igh.
18. **Ow**! **H**ow did you hurt yourself?
19. His **h**omework included **oh**ms.
20. He **h**ates to leave at **ei**ght.

Rhymes for /h/ practice

The blacksmith **h**ammers the **wh**ole day long,
His **h**ammer is **h**eavy, but his arm is strong.
Here comes a **h**orse—what will blacksmith do?
He will **h**ammer out a strong iron shoe.

--Old English Song

Happy **h**earts and **h**appy faces,
Happy play in **h**appy places---
That was **h**ow in ancient ages,
Children grew to kings and sages.

Practice on the go!!

The 19th most frequently used word in English is "his." Just think of all the guys you know, young and old and in-between, and think of all their things. Say: **H**is shoes, **h**is coat, **h**is car, **h**is book, **h**is desk, **h**is family, **h**is work, **h**is house, **h**is vacation, etc.

Chapter 11
Affricate /dʒ/

This sound is a voiced affricate. In plain English, an affricate is a consonant sound that adds a plosive and a friction. (See glossary). In this case, the plosive /d/ combines with the friction /ʒ/.

There are three common problems with this sound. The first is that if the speaker does not voice this sound, a /tʃ/ "ch" will result, so "joke" will sound like "choke." The second is a failure to start this sound with a "d." That will make it sound like a /ʒ/ "zh." The third is in making it sound like the glide that starts the word "yes." This is a common problem for Spanish ESL speakers, because in the Spanish language, that is the way the spelled letter "j" is pronounced.

Pronunciation tips

If, when practicing, you notice your /dʒ/ sounds like a /tʃ/ ("ch"), make sure you start humming as you say this sound. If your /dʒ/ sounds like a /ʒ/ ("zh"), make sure you are starting this sound with a /d/. If you sound like the glide in "**yes**," you need first the /d/ sound and then release the tongue pressure only slightly while continuing to hum.

Spelling tip

The usual spelling for this sound is the letter "j," but sometimes a "g."

Contrastive pairs

/dʒ/	/tʃ/	/ʒ/	/j/
joke	choke	zhoke*	yoke
junk	chunk	zhunk*	yunk*
jump	chump	zhump*	yump*
jest	chest	zhest*	yest*
badge	batch	bazh*	
bridges	britches	brizhes*	briyes*

Practice words

1. jacket	10. jab	19. cage	28. engine
2. jam	11. jazz	20. change	29. ginger
3. jar	12. jest	21. edge	30. magic
4. jelly	13. jet	22. language	31. manager
5. joy	14. join	23. large	32. register
6. juice	15. joke	24. orange	33. agent
7. jump	16. judge	25. page	34. imagine
8. just	17. bridge	26. age	35. logic
9. gem	18. cabbage	27. badge	36. major

Practice sentences

1. Oops! Is that **j**elly on your **j**acket?
2. Flavor the sauce with **gi**nger **j**uice.
3. Let's **j**oin in the **j**oke.
4. I'd like a lar**ge** oran**ge** juice.
5. Can you ima**gi**ne the lo**gi**c of this langua**ge**?
6. Does **J**u**dge** **J**udy like **j**azz?
7. **J**ust let me mark my pa**ge** and I'll **j**oin you.
8. Turn off the en**gi**ne at the e**dge** of the bri**dge**.
9. Did you re**gi**ster with the a**ge**nt at the lo**dge**?
10. Give her a **j**ar of **j**am.

Contrastive pairs in practice sentences

1. It's no **j**oke to **ch**oke.
2. This **ch**unk of metal is **j**unk.
3. Only a **ch**ump would **j**ump from here.
4. They fell for the **j**est about his treasure **ch**est.
5. The baking judge put on her ba**dge** to test my bat**ch** of cookies.

Rhyme for /dʒ/ practice

Joy is like a magic cup
I lift it to the sky,
And all the more I offer up,
The fuller joy have I.

Tongue twister for /dʒ/ practice

Can you imagine an imaginary menagerie manager
imagining managing an imaginary menagerie?

Practice on the go!!

The 129th most commonly used word in English is **just**.

Just let me know. Just when will it be ready? Just wait a minute. That's just right. That's just wonderful. That's just what I wanted. It's just your cup of tea. In just how many other phrases can you think of using just?

Chapter 12
Semi-vowel /l/

Most languages have an initial /l/ sound, and for most ESL speakers, it doesn't present too much trouble, until it gets mixed up with /r/ (for most Japanese and Chinese speakers of English) or /n/ (for English speakers from southern China). Some languages, including Portuguese and most Asian languages, do not have /l/ at the ends of words.

Pronunciation tip

To produce the sound, hold your tongue-tip lightly behind your upper front teeth and hum. Most ESL speakers learned English via the British method, which calls for a "darker" /l/, produced by retracting the tongue-tip quite a bit further back along the hard palate from behind the upper front teeth. The tongue position for the North American style is in the same spot as the tongue-tip for the sounds of /t/, /d/, and /n/, but held there more lightly, and longer. When making the /l/ sound, be sure to let the sound flow along the sides of your tongue, so hold only the tip of your tongue at your upper gum line.

When the /l/ sound occurs at the ends of words, e.g. ball, fill, and smile, ESL speakers from Asia, Portugal and Brazil often have difficulty elevating the tongue-tip and keeping their voices on long enough for their listeners to hear the final /l/, since your languages don't have words that end in /l/. For you, I have included special practice tips that will help.

It will help to keep your /l/ sounding distinct from your /r/ if you realize that the tongue is held tensely for /r/ and loosely for /l/. Then too, the tongue is working toward the back of the mouth for /r/ and toward the front for /l/. When you practice with a mirror, you will not see much difference between /l/ and /n/, but you'll see a great difference between /l/ and /r/.

Contrastive pairs

/l/	/n/	/l/	/r/
let	net	link	rink
lot	knot (not)	late	rate
line	nine	lake	rake
light	night	blue	brew
low	know (no)	flight	fright
		towel	tower
		appeal	appear
		goal	gore

Practice words

1. land
2. last
3. lawn
4. leave
5. left
6. let
7. like
8. little
9. live
10. look
11. love
12. alarm
13. believe
14. belong
15. careless
16. ability
17. solid
18. silence
19. all
20. bell
21. call
22. pull
23. school
24. small
25. fill
26. tell
27. will
28. play
29. please
30. black
31. blue
32. class
33. clean
34. glow
35. flight
36. slow

Special practice phrases for final /l/: Asian and Portuguese Languages

Because your languages don't contain words ending in the /l/ sound, but do contain words beginning with /l/, try linking these phrases, gradually using only one /l/ sound to link, and then drop the second word. Say "tailight", emphasizing the "l". Say it several times, and then drop the "ight" part of the word. Anticipate the second part of the word, but don't say it.

Linking /l/ phrases:

tail light
cell line
table linens
real lace
candle light
little lady
school lawn
small lad
fall leaves
all letters
small lawn

Practice sentences

1. He left his ball at school.
2. I believe she was careless with her doll.
3. We all belong to this land.
4. I live in a solid house with a small lawn.
5. A look of love will tell all.
6. Small blue flowers covered the hillside.
7. Please be careful, you'll be black and blue!
8. Drive slowly in a school zone.
9. I'd better fill the tank before I leave.
10. This flight will tell whether she has the ability.

Contrastive pairs in practice sentences

/r/ and /l/ blend contrasts

1. The clown wore a crown.
2. Throw those old frames on the flames.
3. They cut off their braids with their blades.
4. Pry off the plywood.
5. A crash of thunder sounds like a clash of cymbals.
6. The crowd ran from the cloud.
7. The pituitary is a grand gland.
8. A groom shouldn't look gloomy.
9. I dropped my glass in the grass.
10. The diver didn't blink at the brink of the cliff.
11. Sweep the blooms with the broom.
12. She put a plank over the food for a prank.
13. The coach prayed for a good play.
14. I brewed the tea in the blue pot.
15. Do you want flank steaks or frankfurters?
16. Brew some coffee! We are blue with cold!!
17. The growing child is glowing with health

Final /l/ vs. final /r/ contrasts

1. I left my towel at the tower.
2. It does appear that he will appeal.
3. The goal of the bull is to gore the Matador.
4. We had a beer on Beale Street.
5. She rode her mare to get the mail.
6. They were a pair of pale faces after the shock.

7. Don't lift that ba**l**e with your ba**r**e hands!
8. Coa**l** comes from the co**r**e of the mine.
9. The ca**r** is mi**r**ed a mi**l**e from here.
10. The wa**ll** is dedicated to wa**r** victims.

Distinguish /l/ from /n/

1. The fishermen **l**et down their **n**ets.
2. I didn't **kn**ow I was **l**ow on gas.
3. What is the **n**ame of the horse that went **l**ame?
4. I u**nl**ocked the door when I heard her **kn**ock.
5. We bought a new **n**ight-**l**ight.
6. We have **n**ot had a **l**ot of sunshine.
7. **L**ook in the breakfast **n**ook.
8. Did **L**ee twist his **kn**ee when he fell?
9. When it **sn**ows, the traffic is **sl**ow.
10. We **n**eed two weeks **l**ead-time.
11. The **l**ine is **n**ine feet long.
12. He parked his **L**ear Jet **n**ear the hanger.
13. We'll go **l**oon hunting this after**n**oon.
14. There will be enough **sl**ack time to get a **sn**ack.
15. They were caught **sn**ooping around his **sl**oop.

The Night Light (for /l/ vs. /n/ contrast)

You've no need to light a night-light
On a light night like tonight,
For a night-light's light's a slight light,
And tonight's a night that's light.

When a night's light, like tonight's light,
It is really not quite right
To light night-lights with their slight lights
On a light night like tonight.

Tongue twister for /l/ vs. /r/

The **cr**ow **fl**ew over the **r**iver with a **l**ump of **r**aw **l**iver.

My favorite song for practicing the final /l/ is SMILE, the theme song from Charlie Chaplin's movie "Modern Times." I was not able to secure permission for reprinting it here, but perhaps you'd like to search for it yourself either by Internet, at the library, or your favorite music store.

Practice on the go!!

If distinguishing /l/ from /n/ is your difficulty, then try "**Let's n**ot _____."
Examples: **Let's n**ot rush, ___worry, ___go, ____be afraid, _____leave too soon, _____
__scare her. If distinguishing /l/ from /r/ is the trouble, try "I'd **l**ike to w**r**ite _____."
Examples: _____a letter, _____ a song, _____, a poem, _____an article,
_____a note, _____a message, _____an editorial.

Chapter 13
Consonant /r/

The /r/ consonant is a sound that occurs in most languages, but with broad variations. Many languages such as Italian, Russian, and the Indian languages, use the tip of the tongue to trill or "flap" the /r/. In Asian languages, there is often no clear distinction made between /r/ and /l/.

Pronunciation tip

The American /r/ is produced with the back sides of the tongue rubbing against the inside of the upper molars. Once there, you hum with open lips that are not at all rounded. In fact, it's best to spread them into a smile!

Spelling tip

Spelled "r" is pronounced /r/. The funny thing is that there are some words that begin with a "w" spelling in front of the "r" and the "w" is silent. Examples are wring, wrong, wrist, and write.

Contrastive pairs

/r/	/w/	/l/
read	weed	lead
road		load
rues	woos	lose
rise	wise	lies
reek	week	leek
rink	wink	link
rate	wait	late
rare	ware	lair

rake	wake	lake
red	wed	led

Practice words

1. race	10. rib	19. around	28. remedy
2. ran	11. road (rode)	20. arrest	29. radio
3. read	12. rob	21. every	30. river
4. red	13. room	22. raisin	31. random
5. right (write)	14. wrap (rap)	23. reptile	32. ride
6. ride	15. wreck	24. rapid	33. rice
7. rain	16. rodeo	25. recipe	34. rose
8. run	17. role (roll)	26. record	35. rust
9. round	18. already	27. reason	36. rock

Practice sentences

1. Don't **race** a**r**ound the **r**iver.
2. Stay on the **r**ight side of the **r**oad.
3. I al**r**eady put **r**aisins in the **r**ecipe.
4. W**r**ap the **r**obe a**r**ound you.
5. Stop **r**unning a**r**ound the **r**oom!
6. That **r**usty **r**adio is a w**r**eck.
7. **R**ick wore a **r**ed shirt to the **r**odeo.
8. Give me one good **r**eason to throw that **r**ock.
9. Were the **r**obberies **r**andom?
10. What **r**emedy is there for **r**ust on **r**oses?

Contrastive pairs in sentences

/r/ vs. /l/

1. I left my **r**ake at the **l**ake.
2. She carried a heavy **l**oad down the **r**oad.
3. Don't **w**ait; at this **r**ate you're going to be **late**!
4. After the **r**aid, they **l**aid down their weapons.
5. She lost a **l**ink from her necklace at the **r**ink.
6. A beautiful valley **l**ies just beyond that **r**ise.
7. Don't **r**ip your **l**ip on that broken glass.
8. Get **r**id of that old **l**id.
9. We **r**ode home and un**l**oaded the car.
10. They found a **r**are albino lion in his **l**air.
11. **R**ick! Don't **l**ick icing from the spoon!
12. There's a **l**ot of **r**otten fruit at the bottom of the barrel.
13. Turn **r**ight at the next **l**ight.

14. The **r**ed clown **l**ed the parade.

15. It took a **l**ong time to find what was **wr**ong.

16. The storm left a tree **l**imb along the **r**im of the canyon.

/r/ vs. /w/

17. The cute boy at the roller **r**ink **w**inked at her.

18. That **r**are piece of silver**w**are is worth a king's ransom

19. **W**ake up and help me find the **r**ake.

20. **R**ead the label before you use the **w**eed killer.

/r/ vs. /l/ vs. /w/

21. Before I start to **r**ead, you'd better **l**ead me to the **w**eed patch.

22. I've been harvesting **l**eeks all **w**eek, so my hands **r**eek.

23. They were **l**ed through the **r**ed rose arbor to be **w**ed.

See Chapter 12 for r-blends vs. l-blends

Tongue twister for /r/ practice

Round and **r**ound the **r**ugged **r**ock the **r**agged **r**ascal **r**an!

Practice on the go!!

"Write" is the 64th most frequently used word in English. In case that doesn't sound very frequent to you, you might like to know that any in the top 100 are likely to be used several times every day. Because the word "right" (#145 on the list) is a homophone, you will be getting more value for your "on the go" practice moments. Think of the things we write, and say them aloud during spare moments throughout the day. I'll get you started:

Write your name. Write a letter. Write the report. Write to me! Write the alphabet. Write it down! Write the serial number. Write a check.

Or:

Right you are! Turn right. Right side. She's right. Does that look right?

Part II--Vowels

Introduction to Vowels

Vowels are speech sounds produced by varying positions of the speech organs, the jaw, tongue, teeth, lips, and soft palate, with very little pressure or obstruction to the breath stream, unlike that for the consonants. All vowels are voiced, which means the larynx is vibrating.

Bill Bryson, in his entertaining and enlightening <u>The Mother Tongue: English & How It Got That Way</u>, says, "If there is one thing certain about English pronunciation it is that there is almost nothing certain about it." I'm afraid this is true even more for the vowels than for the consonants.

The vowels are generally classified as front, central and back vowels. This is because the tongue is bunched toward the front of the mouth for the vowels /i/, /ɪ/, /e/, /ɛ/, and /æ/; the center of the mouth for / ɝ, ɚ, ʌ, ə/; and the back of the mouth for / u, ʊ, o, ɔ, a/.

In addition to the positioning of the tongue in the mouth, the other important factor for making each vowel sound distinct from the other is how tensely or how relaxed the tongue muscles are held. For each of the front, central and back groups, the first one listed requires the most tension. Each succeeding vowel in the order listed requires slightly less tension. The last one of each group has the least tension. I mention this not because I expect you to pass a course in phonetics, but because I think the overall concept can be useful as we discuss the remedy for problems you may be having. For example, if you intend to say "ship" but your listener hears "sheep" you would fix that by relaxing your jaw so that your tongue relaxes into the correct position. Try that now. Keep it in mind as you work through the vowel sections that apply to you.

Chapter 14
Vocalic r, /ɝ, ɚ/

The r sound behaves as a vowel when it's in the middle or at the end of a word. That's why it's called vocalic. It's an impressionable sound. It likes to take on influences from surrounding sounds. It's unstable. Maybe this is why it causes so much difficulty—even to younger native speakers. It is often the last sound learned, and typically comprises the lion's share of the school speech therapist's caseload. In British English, this sound is produced almost as a prolongation of it's preceding vowel sound. Most ESL speakers who learned English in their native countries learned the British style of English pronunciation.

Pronunciation tip

Rub the back sides of your tongue against the insides of your upper molars and hum.

Practice tip

For those who can make a consonant /r/ but struggle with /ɝ/ and /ɚ/, try the sentences below. Make the vocalic r, that's the one at the end of the word, blend into the consonant r that starts the next word. You can take the two-word phrase, e.g. "river road," and ignore the last r in river, but concentrate on the first r in road. That should give you "riveroad," "betterain," "paperoses," etc. Try saying each of these a few times, and then gradually leave off the "oad," "ain," and "oses" parts until you are left with "river," "better," "paper," with a good solid r at the end. For that matter, if you already have a firm vocalic r, but struggle with your consonant r, you can reverse this process. In this case, you would gradually drop the first part of the linked phrase until you are left with "road," "rain," and "roses."

Practice sentences for vocalic /ɚ/ to consonant /r/ transitions

1. We drove along Rive**r R**oad.
2. It bette**r r**ain.
3. Beatrix Potter wrote "Pete**r R**abbit."
4. She made pape**r r**oses.
5. She wore a blue hai**r r**ibbon.
6. Our canoe hit a bigge**r r**ock.
7. His new car is fi**r**e **r**ed.
8. We listened to the Tige**r R**ag.
9. The boys inflated the rubbe**r r**aft.
10. There was a ca**r wr**eck on Interstate 40.
11. The bea**r r**an into the forest.
12. Madison has an annual rive**r r**ace.
13. Our dog loves an ea**r r**ub.
14. The moto**r r**an too hard.

Spelling tip

The rule is that all "r" spellings should be pronounced. The exception is for some French borrow words such as "dossier" where the "r" is silent.

Contrastive pairs

/ɝ/	/ʊ/	/ʌ/
shirk	shook	shuck
word	would	
heard	hood	HUD
curb		cub
burg		bug

Practice words

Say these as though there were no other vowel. For example, #1 is "rrth," # 2 is "rrly," # 3 is "rrn," # 9 is "srr," #15 is "shrrt", etc.

1. earth	10. her	19. word
2. early	11. were	20. work
3. earn	12. curb	21. worm
4. earnest	13. dirt	22. thermos
5. urban	14. hurt	23. germ
6. urgent	15. shirt	24. burn
7. herb	16. bird	25. worse
8. urge	17. third	26. thirsty
9. sir	18. heard	27. perfume

Practice sentences

1. Are you in **ear**nest s**ir**?
2. We w**ere** parked at the c**ur**b.
3. I h**ear**d a b**ir**d outside my window.
4. If you're th**ir**sty, there is a th**er**mos of lemonade.
5. Has **ur**ban pollution w**or**sened?
6. He **ur**ged me to be **ear**ly.
7. We w**ere** h**ur**t by h**er** harsh w**or**ds.
8. S**ear**ch cool, moist d**ir**t for **ear**thw**or**ms.
9. He **ear**ned enough to buy his own sh**ir**t.
10. This is the th**ir**d time I b**ur**ned the toast.

Practice sentences for contrastive pairs

1. I heard he's working for HUD.
2. Is that a bear cub at the c**ur**b?
3. This w**or**d would be better.
4. She sh**oo**k her fist at him when she found he had sh**ir**ked his duty of sh**u**cking the corn.

Old proverb for /ɝ/ practice

The **ear**ly b**ir**d catches the w**or**m.

Practice on the go!!

The 39th most frequently used word in English is "**were.**" We were _____ (going, busy, tired, happy, late, early, not home, surprised, hungry, thirsty, playing cards, and so on.

ɚ–diphthongs are combinations of the /ɚ/ with its preceding vowel. In other words, you must sound both the vowel and its following /ɚ/ as a unit. Notice that this is not like the practice words above, where you are sounding the /ɝ/ only.

r-diphthongs ( )=rank order. See **notations** in the Introduction.

1. there (41) *
2. your (45)
3. their (53) *
4. more (76)
5. part (104)
6. where (110)
7. year (117)
8. form (130)
9. before (143)
10. port (165)
11. large (166)
12. near (196)
13. four (218)
14. farm (230)
15. hard (231)
16. start (232)
17. north (250)
18. mark (268)
19. car (274)
20. care (276)
21. carry (279)
22. hear (292)
23. horse (293)
24. sure (294)
25. short (327)
26. order (338)
27. hour (353)
28. morning (375)
29. toward (380)
30. war (381)
31. appear (391)
32. dark (410)
33. star (416)
34. warm (439)
35. clear (446)
36. course (454)
37. force (456)
38. record (470)

39. heart (506)
40. arm (513)
41. pair (526)
42. square (535)
43. art (539)
44. forest (552)
45. store (556)
46. board (569)
47. bear (592)
48. organ (673)
49. poor (686)
50. yard (722)
51. wear (737)
52. garden (738)
53. corner (782)
54. party (783)
55. chair (793)
56. sharp (803)
57. compare (812)
58. fear (823)
59. chart (852)
60. particular (859)
61. born (872)
62. quart (874)
63. require (859)
64. prepare (894)
65. forward (922)
66. score (926)
67. card (933)
68. shore (954)
69. chord (962)
70. share (966)
71. charge (970)
72. bar (972)
73. market (978)
74. dear (982)
75. support (987)

*homophones

Chapter 15
Front Vowel /ɪ/

This front vowel may be the sound of English that is most frequently mispronounced by all speakers of English as a second language. The mistake is that they pronounce it as a "long i" or "ee" sound instead of a short. When small children in the United States are pretending to be from someplace else they will say "leetle" for "little" and "beeg" for "big." Their ears have already told them about this difference.

Pronunciation tip

To keep from making this mistake, just start as though you were going to say /i/ but lower your jaw slightly and relax your mouth, to achieve the /ɪ/ sound.

/ɪ/	/i/
bit	beat
dip	deep
bill	Beale
pick	peak (peek)
ship	sheep
itch	each

Common spellings

Many people ask me how to tell which is which. Usually, go for the /ɪ/ if the word or the stressed syllable of the word is spelled with a single "i." Don't expect to use the sound /i/ unless the word is spelled with two vowels together, such as "ee" or "ea."

Practice Words

1. if	12. big	23. ship
2. in	13. did	24. tissue
3. is	14. give	25. chicken
4. it	15. him (hymn)	26. figure
5. itch	16. milk	27. little
6. ignore	17. pig	28. trip
7. image	18. six	29. scissors
8. impact	19. will	30. mission
9. impel	20. bill	31. bridge
10. index	21. fish	32. swim
11. irritate	22. lid	33. dinner

Practice Sentences

1. His sister has six pigs.
2. Tim gave a ticket to the little girl.
3. Will you give him some milk?
4. If you are sick of chicken, order fish.
5. Bill will pin the note to the bulletin board.
6. Is that your ship?
7. She tossed a coin from the wishing bridge.
8. It's too chilly to swim.
9. Linda! You should never run with scissors!
10. We'll have a simple dish for dinner.

Contrastive pairs practice sentences:

1. I live here; I leave at seven.
2. John made a bid on the beads.
3. Take a dip, but don't go too deep.
4. Susie bit into the beet.
5. A bin of beans was next to the rice.
6. He tried to kill the marlin by the keel.
7. Pick the berries at their peak.
8. The teens packed tins of fruit.
9. I'm afraid they'll deem us dim witted.
10. Did he sign the deed?
11. I got a good deal on dill at the farmer's market.
12. He's not too keen on meeting her kin.
13. The constant peal of the bell made me take a pill.
14. Aren't you going to eat it?
15. The eel in my aquarium is ill.

16. **I**s there any **ea**se in the workload?
17. They carried p**ea**t from the p**i**t.
18. What does it cost to sh**i**p the sh**ee**p?
19. She s**ee**ks highway s**i**x.
20. We took the m**ea**l to the m**i**ll.
21. L**ea**d me to the l**i**d.
22. The D**ea**n heard the d**i**n from the study hall.
23. I have a ceramic s**ea**l on my s**i**ll.
24. W**i**ll you take the wh**ee**l?
25. I put calamine lotion on **ea**ch **i**tch
26. **I**ck!! How can she **e**ke out a living here?
27. These shoes don't f**i**t my f**ee**t.
28. The boy in the gr**ee**n shirt has a funny gr**i**n.
29. R**ea**d the papers, and then get r**i**d of them.
30. I tried to sl**i**p off to sl**ee**p.
31. I found his h**ee**l print on the h**i**ll.
32. I kn**i**t him a n**ea**t sweater.
33. The sl**ee**pers wore sl**i**ppers.

Tongue twisters for /ɪ/ practice

Give me the g**i**ft of a gr**i**p top sock.

Six thick thistle sticks. Six thick thistles stick.

Is this your sister's sixth zither, sir?

Mrs. Smith's Fish is delicious. (Don't forget the /ɪ/ in Mrs.-missez).

Quick kiss. Quicker kiss.

Tim, the thin twin tinsmith

Which witch wished which wicked wish?

Six silly sisters sell silk to six silly misters

Practice on the go!!

Take every occasion throughout the day to observe the world around you, and say, "This is a _____ (e.g. windy day, lot of traffic, slippery street, crooked road, crowded room, and so on.)

The 7th most frequently used word in English is "**is**."

The 19th most frequently used word is "**his**."

The 25th most frequently used is "**this**."

With such high frequency rankings for all of these, your time is well spent in rehearsing them over and over until you've developed the habit. Another useful ***on the go*** practice phrase is, "This **is his** _____." Fill in the blank with everything you can think of. This is his book. This is his pen. This is his desk. This is his son. This is his daughter. This is his wife. This is his car. This is his house. You can go on all day. The more you say these, the easier they become, and the more likely they will be to happen naturally when you are not thinking about it.

Caution! "This" and "these" are not homophones! Say "this" with the short i, /ɪ/ and "these" with the long i, /i/. The pronunciation of the "s" at the end is different too. That is addressed in chapter 8.

Chapter 16
The "short u" vowel /ʊ/

This back vowel has the same relationship with the "long u" as the "short i" has from the "long i" in the previous section. It too presents problems for most ESL speakers.

Pronunciation tip

Just as for the difference between long and short i, the tongue position is nearly the same for long and short u. You simply start from the long u sound (oo as in too, tooth, goose) and relax the entire mouth. Relax your lips from a tight circle to a loose oval shape. Relax your jaw; open your mouth just a bit more than for long u.

Spelling tip

A word of caution! Never trust a double o (oo) spelling! Some are pronounced with a long u and some with a short. Usually, -ool endings are pronounced long (school, tool, pool,) and –ook endings are pronounced with short u (book, took, look, forsook).

Contrastive pairs

/ʊ/	/u/
pull	pool
look	Luke
full	fool
hood	who'd
stood	stewed
should	shooed
could	cooed

Practice words

1. would	10. pull
2. look	11. stood
3. could	12. full
4. good	13. foot
5. put	14. push
6. should	15. cook
7. book	16. poor
8. took	17. plural
9. wood	18. sugar

Practice sentences

1. I **too**k a go**o**d b**oo**k from the shelf.
2. She p**u**t the w**oo**d on the fire.
3. L**oo**k at the f**u**ll s**u**gar bowl.
4. The p**oo**r c**oo**k st**oo**d over the stove.
5. I c**ou**ld push if you w**ou**ld p**u**ll.
6. The gymnast st**oo**d on one f**oo**t.
7. We t**oo**k a l**oo**k at the neighborh**oo**d.
8. What a go**o**d c**oo**kie!
9. There is a br**oo**k beyond those b**u**shes.
10. I left my w**oo**l sweater on the w**oo**den table.

Contrastive pairs in practice sentences

1. P**u**ll the boat into the p**oo**l.
2. L**oo**k at Luke.
3. C**ou**ld you hear him if he c**oo**ed?
4. She st**oo**d by while I st**e**wed the meat.
5. I sh**ou**ld have sh**oo**ed those rabbits.
6. W**ho**'d look under the h**oo**d?
7. You can't f**oo**l me, that tank isn't f**u**ll.

Tongue twister for /ʊ/, the short u sound

How much w**oo**d w**ou**ld a w**oo**dchuck chuck if a w**oo**dchuck c**ou**ld chuck w**oo**d?

Practice on the go

Think about the things you'd like to do. "I **cou**ld _____" go on a picnic, take a walk, plan my vacation, visit my friend, and so on.

"Would" is the 63rd most frequently used word in English. "Could" is the 78th most frequent. What w**ou**ld you do if you c**ou**ld? I would go swimming if I could. I would go scuba diving if I could. I would go hiking if I could. I would rest if I could. I would go skydiving if I could. Try these and make up your own.

Chapter 17
Back Vowel /a/

Production of this sound is the most relaxed of all the sounds of English. It is made the furthest back in your mouth. It's as though you've just come home from a hard and hectic day, you've taken off your shoes and leaned back in your favorite chair. "Ahhh."

A mistake here could make you sound like you've said she was robed when you meant she was robbed.

Spelling tip

Many words spelled with a single "a" are pronounced with this sound. Father and want are common examples. The problem that most ESL speakers have with this sound is that they think too logically. I say this because most words that are spelled with a single "o" in the stressed syllable of the word have "ah" as their vowel sound. Yep. You read that correctly. Spell with an "o"; pronounce with an /a/. Quite a leap of faith isn't it? If you are skeptical, listen closely to your American friends. What do you hear when they say, "Good job" or "Thanks a lot"? If you are wondering whether this is another difference from British style, you are absolutely correct.

Contrastive pairs

/a/	/o/
cop	cope
pop	Pope
mop	mope
rot	rote
not	note
nod	node
rod	road (rode)
rob	robe

Practice words

1. honest	10. box	19. prom
2. honor	11. toxic	20. crop
3. olive	12. project	21. c**o**tton
4. father	13. opera	22. forg**o**tten
5. want	14. top	23. rotten
6. bomb	15. not (knot)	24. m**o**nitor
7. Tom	16. spot	25. lobster
8. Bob	17. lot	26. corr**o**borate
9. pop	18. prop	27. problem

By the way, do you know why I bolded the "o" in numbers 21, 22, 24, and 26? That's in case you are not sure which "o" is in the stressed syllable.

Practice sentences

1. T**o**m wa**n**ts an **o**live.
2. B**o**b wa**n**ts a sp**o**t on the fut**o**n.
3. M**o**lly wa**n**ts to take her d**o**ll to the **o**pera.
4. Scarcity of t**o**p quality is a c**o**mmon pr**o**blem.
5. My f**a**ther has a new j**o**b.
6. I'll be h**o**nored to lead the pr**o**ject.
7. They are m**o**nitoring the l**o**bsters.
8. Did they spray t**o**xins on the c**o**tton cr**o**p?
9. The duckling with the t**o**pkn**o**t is cute.
10. The fruit in this b**o**x is r**o**tten.

Contrastive pairs in practice sentences

1. Don't m**o**pe about using the m**o**p.
2. That's n**o**t the n**o**te I wanted.
3. The r**o**bber wore a r**o**be.
4. The r**o**d broke on the bumpy r**o**ad.
5. I saw him n**o**d when he found the n**o**de.
6. P**o**p was excited to meet the P**o**pe.

Tongue twister for the /a/ vowel

If one doctor doctors another doctor, does the doctor who doctors the doctor doctor the doctor the way the doctor he is doctoring doctors?

Practice on the go!!

The 30th most frequently used word in English is "hot." While you are driving to and from work, or running errands, think of all the things that can be hot. Remember, it only counts if you say these aloud:

Hot tea, hot coffee, hot engine, hot weather, hot stove, hot pavement, hot meal, hot water, etc.

Chapter 18
Central Vowel /ʌ/

This vowel is classified as "central" because it is made with the bulk of the tongue in the central part of the mouth. If you have ever made the sound of hesitation, "Uh, I think so." "Uh, I guess I'll have coffee," this is the sound we're dealing with in this section. I have seldom encountered an ESL speaker from any mother tongue who did not have some confusion about this sound. The most typical confusion is with the vowel /a/ "ah."

Usual spelling for this sound is "u" but occasionally it's spelled with an "o" and can even be spelled "ou" as in "young."

Contrastive pairs

/ʌ/	/a/
bum	bomb
cut	cot
duck	dock
sum (some)	psalm
pup	pop
shut	shot
cup	cop
cub	cob

Practice words

1. other	10. oven	19. just
2. ugly	11. ultimate	20. glove
3. umbrella	12. ultra	21. love
4. uncle	13. upper	22. mother
5. under	14. usher	23. brother
6. unless	15. but	24. much
7. until	16. come	25. husband
8. up	17. cut	26. truck
9. us	18. jump	27. tongue

Practice sentences

1. My mother bought the other umbrella.
2. His uncle is working under the truck.
3. Your brother loves that ugly puppy.
4. Her husband doesn't think much of her new gloves.
5. Unless you see an usher, don't come.
6. Just clean the upper oven.
7. Don't jump until he cuts the rope.
8. The ultimate solution is up to us.
9. Do you think your husband will jump at this chance?
10. Why did you put that duck in your trunk?

Contrastive pairs in practice sentences

1. How did the bum get a bomb?
2. Sue cut her finger on the old cot.
3. A beautiful duck is swimming around the dock.
4. Dan memorized some psalms.
5. The cute pup popped out of the box.
6. Shut the door. I heard a shot!
7. Give the cop a cup of coffee.
8. There's a bear cub chewing on corncobs.

Tongue twister for /ʌ/ vowel practice

I met the other three brothers of their mother's brother's side.

Rhyme for /ʌ/ vowel practice

For every evil **u**nder the s**u**n,
There is a remedy or there is n**o**ne.
If there be **o**ne, try and find it;
If there be n**o**ne never mind it.

Practice on the go!!

The 2nd most frequently used word in English is **of.** The 34th is **some**.

a glass of water, a cup of tea, a glass of juice, a piece of toast, a piece of pie, a piece of cake, a loaf of bread, a carton of eggs , a bottle of cola, a stick of gum, a box of candy, a bowl of soup, a dish of ice cream, plenty of time, a quart of milk, etc. or some bread, some milk, some eggs, some juice, some toast, some pie, some candy, some gum, some soup, some time, some tea, some coffee, some water, some flowers, etc.

Chapter 19
Front Vowel, /ɛ/

This is a "front vowel", meaning that the tongue is bunched more toward the front of the mouth to produce it. The usual trouble people encounter with this vowel is that they have difficulty hearing and producing the difference between /ɛ/ and its next-door neighbor to the South, the vowel /æ/. Some ESL speakers also have trouble distinguishing it from its next-door neighbor to the North, the /e/ vowel. (See Introduction to vowels).

Now stay with me for a minute while I explain why I say neighbor, North, and South. Your mouth opening and the position of your jaw, along with the height of your tongue position are what make vowels change from one sound to another. The five front vowels are /i/, /ɪ/, /e/, /ɛ/, and /æ/. Of these, the tongue is higher and tighter, or tenser, for /i/ and gradually lower and less tense for each of the others in the order I have listed them here.

Pronunciation tip

You may find it easier to try making these by opening your mouth slightly more for each, so that the tongue follows by lowering. That's what I mean when I say that /ɛ/ is just South of /e/ and just North of /æ/.

Spelling tip

Usually spelled with a single "e" but can be spelled "ea" as in head and bread, with an "a" as in any and its extensions—anywhere, anybody, etc. Note also the special cases "said" and "been" which are different than British English.

Contrastive pairs

/ɛ/	/e/	/æ/
men	main (mane, Maine)	man
peck		pack
shell	shale	shall
wed	wade	
hem		ham
beg		bag
head		had
medicine		Madison
edge	age	
net		gnat
let	late	
tell	tail (tale)	
debt	date	

Practice words

1. any	10. extra	19. bed	28. beg
2. edge	11. edit	20. dress	29. deck
3. egg	12. elegant	21. guess	30. hem
4. elephant	13. elevate	22. help	31. hen
5. elm	14. elk	23. let	32. leg
6. else	15. enter	24. men	33. met
7. end	16. entry	25. said	34. neck
8. engine	17. etch	26. them	35. pen
9. every	18. excellent	27. well	36. web

Practice sentences

1. Does **a**nybody want to help paint the deck?
2. The **e**legant dress has a narrow hem.
3. **E**very hen sat on a nest of eggs.
4. **A**ny extra help will be welcome.
5. Let the men at the entrance help you.
6. Ben's engine is the eleventh entry.
7. I g**ue**ss the elephant needs medicine for her leg.
8. The doctor s**ai**d* to elevate the head of the bed.
9. **E**very web page has b**ee**n* edited.
10. What **e**lse can she use to edge the neck of the dress?

*Yes. Unlike British, North American Standard pronunciation uses the /ɛ/ vowel. This has come as a surprise to nearly every ESL speaker I've ever worked with.

Contrastive pairs in practice sentences

/ɛ/ **vs.** /æ/
1. I dropped ham on my hem.
2. She begged for a bag of candy.
3. I had a **headache**.
4. We bought the medicine on **Ma**dison Avenue
5. They called him a man among men.
6. A gnat is too small for that net.
7. Shall we look for shells?
8. Pack a peck of strawberries.

/ɛ/ **vs.** /e/
9. They found shells among the shale.
10. Those men come from **Maine**.
11. Tell us a happy tale.
12. Let's not be late.
13. He'll be out of debt by that date.
14. In this **age** you need an **edge**.

Tongue twister for /ɛ/ practice

Lesser leather never weathered wetter weather better.

Practice on the go!!

The 42nd most frequently used word in English is when.

When are you going? When are you coming? When is your vacation? When does the meeting start? When did it happen? When do you want it? When will dinner be ready?

Practice these and make up some of your own.

Special tip for French ESL speakers

Due to pronunciation conventions in French, the following –en- spellings often present challenges when encountered in English. Use the /ɛ/ vowel for the following:

1. pretense   They made a pretense of paying attention.
2. presence   Your presence will be appreciated.
3. present   What a thoughtful present! May I present Mrs. Wood?
4. sense   The sense of smell is important to the enjoyment of food.
5. menace   A neurologist may use a menacing gesture to test a patient's reflexes.
6. pensive   I was in a pensive mood when I wrote that.

7. fence   We'll have to climb the fence to gather blackberries.
8. tense, tension   There was tension in the courtroom before the verdict.
9. dense   The fog was dense this morning.
10. clench   I clenched my jaw at the pain.
11. bench   The player sat on the bench.
12. sequence   Please describe the sequence of events leading up to the accident.
13. convention   The convention hotel houses 900 guests.
14. consequence   The consequence of poor diet is bad health.
15. fundamental(ly)   I'm afraid that theory is fundamentally wrong.
16. identify   They are trying to identify the cause.
17. exponentially   If you don't control weeds in the early spring, they will increase exponentially throughout the growing season.
18. expensive   Do you think these gloves are too expensive?
19. defense   In her defense, I have to say that she is trying.
20. depend   I need a car that I can depend on.
21. send   Send the letter promptly.
22. fend   She's too young and inexperienced to fend for herself.
23. lend   Can you lend me your laptop for the afternoon?
24. portend   I'm afraid those clouds portend an end to our picnic.

Chapter 20
The Most Frequently Used Sound in the English Language—the Schwa /ə/

This sound, besides being the most frequently used sound in English, is also the weakest and most neutral. It appears in nearly every word of two or more syllables, and all words of more than two syllables. It accounts for a great deal of the rhythm of spoken English. It is the sound used for the vowel in the weak syllable of the word, regardless of spelling. In longer words, there can be two or more unstressed syllables and so two or more schwas. Numbers 18, 20, 29, and 33 in the practice words below are examples of two schwas in a word.

Pronunciation tip

The problem that ESL speakers have with schwa is that they pronounce it too strongly, giving it the full value of the spelled vowel. Say it quickly and lightly.

Usual spelling:

Often an "a", but can be any vowel, as long as it's in the unstressed syllable.

There are no contrastive pairs for this sound.

Practice words

1. about	10. awhile	19. soda	28. balloon
2. above	11. abate	20. vanilla	29. banana
3. ago	12. allow	21. china (China)	30. breakfast
4. alive	13. amass	22. data	31. circus
5. along	14. amaze	23. quota	32. company
6. another	15. annoy	24. visa	33. element
7. around	16. appeal	25. zebra	34. necessary
8. asleep	17. attach	26. accident	35. nervous
9. away	18. arena	27. alphabet	36. relative

Practice sentences

(Notice that articles "the" and "a" are both pronounced schwa!)

1. She was about to have a vanilla soda.
2. We were amazed at the appeal of that company.
3. The zebra often represents the last letter of the alphabet.
4. It isn't necessary to amass a fortune.
5. My relatives have applied for a visa.
6. Would you like a banana for breakfast?
7. Another accident will make you nervous.
8. Wait awhile and we'll take a balloon ride.
9. She worked in the circus about ten years ago.
10. Let's look for another way around.

There are no contrastive pairs practice sentences for this sound

A rhyme for schwa /ə/ practice

A swarm of bees in May,
Is worth a load of hay.
A swarm of bees in June,
Is worth a silver spoon.
A swarm of bees in July,
Isn't worth a fly.

Practice on the go!!

Because the most frequently occurring word in the English language is **the**, just look around you and say, "the car, the sky, the tree, the flowers, the leaves, the grass, the street, the building. Do the same thing with the ubiquitous article **a**. "A hat, a key, a book, a desk, a program, a project, a pen, a screen, a monitor, a light, a cup, a spoon, etc.

Please note

The only time the letter "e" in the word "the" is **not** pronounced as schwa is when the next word begins with a vowel **sound**. Then, and only then, should it be pronounced /i/, like "thee." Examples are the orange, the only, the end, the element, the honorable (because of the silent "h"), the unmet need, but the (thuh) universe, because in words such as universe, uniform, and unique, the first sound is the glide /j/, not the vowel /ʌ/. Remember to apply this rule by the first sound of the word—not necessarily the first spelled letter.

Chapter 21
Back Vowel /o/

Common difficulties with this sound are confusing it with /ʌ/, /ɔ/,or /ɑ/, or in stretching it into /oə/.

Spelling tips

The two most common spellings for the vowel sound /o/ are "oa" as in boat and coat, and a single "o" with consonants on either side but with a silent "e" at the end as in phone and code. Other spellings are "oe" as in Joe and toe, and "ow" as in snow and grow.

Contrastive pairs

/o/	/ɔ/	/ɑ/
boat	bought	
tote	taught (taut)	tot
phone	fawn	
bowl	bawl (ball)	
coat	caught	cot
hole (whole)	haul	
coal	call	
code	cawed	cod

Practice words

1. oak	10. odor	19. snow	28. boat
2. oat	11. opal	20. so	29. both
3. oh	12. oval	21. toe	30. don't
4. old	13. go	22. crow	31. home
5. only	14. grow	23. doe (dough)	32. loaf
6. open	15. hello	24. low	33. soap
7. over	16. Joe	25. flow	34. code
8. own	17. know (no)	26. though	35. note
9. ocean	18. show	27. throw	36. soul

Practice sentences

1. Joe rowed his boat under the old oak.
2. Don't go home until you've learned the code.
3. Open the soap and throw it to me.
4. She wrote a note to both of us..
5. Close the stove and open the window.
6. The snow was so cold we only stayed out for an hour.
7. He rode his pony home from the store.
8. Tony will come over after the show.
9. Why did you throw your loaf into the ocean?
10. Did you grow your own oats?

Contrastive pairs in practice sentences

1. Who bought a boat?
2. She taught the tot to tote his toys.
3. Now where did I put my bowling ball?
4. He caught his coat on the cot.
5. Can you haul the whole load?
6. Call for more coal.
7. Is there a code for the shipment of cod?

Old rhyme for /o/ practice:

Old King Cole
was a merry old soul,
and a merry old soul was he.
He called for his pipe,
and he called for his bowl,
and he called for his fiddlers three.

Practice on the go!!

The 27th most frequently used word in English is "or." Think of beverage choices: tea or coffee, milk or juice, Coke or Pepsi, red or white wine, water or lemonade, etc.

Chapter 22
Back Vowel /ɔ/

The most common difficulty ESL speakers have with this vowel is to replace it with it's neighbor to the North /o/ (see vowel introduction) or to take the spelling of some words at face value and pronounce as a diphthong, e.g. "sauce" and "because."

Pronunciation tip

If you've ever heard a North American speaker of English say "aw" when they see a cute baby, human or animal, this is the sound for this vowel. The tongue rises in the back of the mouth and the lips are relaxed and only slightly rounded.

Spelling tip

Note the variations below: ou, au, aw, a

Contrastive pairs

/ɔ/	/au/	/o/
bought	bout	boat
caught		coat
fawn		phone
fall	foul (fowl)	foal
taught (taut)		tote
ball	bowel	bowl
lawn		loan (lone)

Practice words

1. all	10. awful	19. ball
2. also	11. awkward	20. caught
3. almost	12. claw	21. fall
4. already	13. draw	22. hawk
5. office	14. law	23. tall
6. often	15. paw	24. taught
7. ought	16. raw	25. thought
8. author	17. straw	26. walk
9. autumn	18. saw	27. cause

Practice sentences

1. He **ou**ght to study **l**aw.
2. The **au**thor had an **aw**ful th**ough**t.
3. Can you dr**aw** a d**o**g's p**aw**?
4. We love to w**a**lk in the **au**tumn.
5. This meat is **a**lmost r**aw**!
6. The h**aw**k c**au**ght the ball in its cl**aw**.
7. She's **a**lready g**o**ne to her **o**ffice.
8. He **o**ften t**au**ght what he s**aw**.
9. Just bec**au**se he's t**a**ll doesn't mean he's **aw**kward.
10. I dropped my str**aw** in the s**au**ce.

Contrastive pairs in practice sentences

1. After a b**ou**t of flu, he b**ou**ght a b**oa**t.
2. She c**au**ght up her c**oa**t from the chair and left.
3. Sue held her t**o**te bag t**au**ght across her arm.
4. Put down the ph**o**ne and come see this f**aw**n!
5. We'll need a l**oa**n to repair the l**aw**n.

Tongue twisters

I thought a thought.
But the thought I thought wasn't the thought
I thought I thought.

(Good for /ɵ/ practice too. See chapter 5.)

I saw Esau kissing Kate. I saw Esau,
he saw me, and she saw I saw Esau.

The sawingest saw I ever saw saw
was the saw I saw saw in Arkansas.

Practice on the go!!

The 14th most frequently used word in English is "on". Where did you leave your keys? Imagine all the logical and illogical places you may have left your keys.

I left them on the_____. (chair, desk, piano, T.V., table, kitchen counter, bed, nightstand, bookcase, coffee table, lamp table, etc.)

Remember to practice in full sentences, repeating the key word "on" each time.

I've left mine "in" a lot of places too, but that's Chapter 15. You might like to alternate these two sections. Remember, nearly everyone has difficulty with the /ɪ/ vowel.

Chapter 23
/ai/ and /au/ diphthongs

The problem here is the strong tendency to reduce these two-part vowel sounds to one. It seems especially difficult when either of them is followed by an /n/, such as "down" and "bind", so be particularly diligent with your practice of those. Did you say, "It's Don" or "It's down"? Are we in a "bond" or a "bind"?

Pronunciation tip

Make sure you pronounce both the vowels, not just the first /a/ part.

Spelling tip

The /au/ diphthong can be spelled with an "ou" or an "ow." The /ai/ can be spelled with a single "i", as in "find", but is often spelled with silent e at the end of the word as in "mine."

Contrastive pairs

/au/	/a/	/ai/	/a/
found	fond	find	fond
doubt	dot	bind	bond
down	don (Don)	dine	don (Don)
brow	bra	nine	non
noun	non	night	not (knot)

105

Practice words

	/au/			/ai/	
1. hour (our)	10. about		19. eye (I)	28. why
2. ouch	11. around		20. ice	29. tie
3. ounce	12. brown		21. idea	30. sky
4. out	13. count		22. idle	31. cry
5. owl	14. down		23. iris	32. find
6. allow	15. found		24. iron	33. time
7. brow	16. ground		25. aisle (I'll)	34. kind
8. how	17. round		26. ideal	35. mine
9. now	18. town		27. by (buy, bye)	36. line

Practice sentences

1. We'll be there in about an hour.
2. Would you like to go down town?
3. Have you seen a brown cow around here?
4. If you have time, please try to find some irises.
5. This is the ideal time.
6. What kind of iron did you buy?
7. Why don't you put ice on your eye?
8. They finally found the time to visit.
9. It was kind of you to help with the grounds.
10. The racers lined up for the countdown.

Contrastive pairs in practice sentences

1. She's fond of the picture he found.
2. Don came down early.
3. Is this a non count noun?
4. He has doubts that the dot coms will rebound.
5. Donna's mother raised her brow at the purchase of that bra.
6. Let's dine with Don.
7. It's not a night for walking.
8. Is the bond issue binding?
9. Find someone to be fond of.
10. Nine entrants were nonstarters.

A proverb for practicing /au/

If we count the things that don't count, we may fail to count the things that count.

A rhyme for /ai/ practice:

Good-Morrow to you, Valentine!
Curl your locks as I do mine;
Two before and three behind.
Good-morrow to you, Valentine!

And a rhyme for both /au/ and /ai/

Baby moon, 'tis time for bed,
Owlet leaves his nest n**ow**;
Hide your little horned head
In the tw**i**light west n**ow**;
When you're old and r**ou**nd and br**i**ght
You shall stay and sh**i**ne all night.

Practice on the go!!

Think of everyone you know. Say, "Sam went to t**ow**n." "Mary_____." "Paul_____."
Etc. It's time to go. It's time to eat. It's time to leave. It's time to_____, etc.

Appendices

Appendix A

Cues for the Production of Speech Sounds

<u>Sound</u>	<u>Sample words</u>	<u>Cue</u>
/p/	put, apple, keep	Close lips. Force them open with a puff of air.
/b/	ball, able, rub	As for /p/ but add voice.
/m/	man, summer, name	Close lips and hum.
/n/	nose, any, can	Open mouth, place tip of tongue on gum behind upper teeth and add voice
/t/	toe, little, pat	Same as for /n/ but instead of using voice, blow tongue tip away with a puff of air.
/d/	do, shady, red	Same as for /t/ but add voice.
/k/	key, cookie, make	Arch the back of the tongue so that it touches the soft palate. Lower it quickly as you blow.
/g/	go, sugar, egg	Same as for /k/ but add voice.
/ŋ/	___, sing, singer	Same starting position as for /k/ and /g/, but keep your tongue still and send your voice through your nose.
/f/	food, coffee, loaf	Gently bite your bottom lip and blow.
/v/-	vase, ever, love	Same as for /f/ but hum instead of blowing.
/θ/	thin, healthy, both	Touch the edges of your front teeth with the tip of your tongue. Blow gently.

/ð/	the, other, breathe	same as for voiceless /th/ but add voice.
/s/	see, essay, voice	Place the tongue behind the upper teeth just at the gum. Close the teeth lightly and blow down the center of the tongue.
/z/	zoo, easy, please	Same as for /s/ but add voice.
/ʃ/	she, fishing, wish	As for /s/ but draw the tongue back a little and push your lips forward before blowing.
/ʒ/	__, vision, beige	Same as for /ʃ/ but add voice.
/tʃ/	chew, kitchen, lunch	Make the /t/ and the /ʃ at the same time.
/dʒ/	jar, logic, page	Same as for /tʃ/ but add voice
/l/	look, allow, all	Place the tongue-tip on the gum behind the upper teeth. Let your voice escape over the sides of the tongue.
/r,ɚ,ɝ/	red, carry, or	Pretend you have food stuck on the insides of your upper back molars, and you can only get it out by sing the back sides of your tongue. Add voice.
/h/	he, perhaps,___	Sigh without voice.
/w/	wet, somewhere	Round the lips just slightly less that you would for whistling. Move them quickly to the next sound.
/j/	you, value, __	Begin to say the vowel sound "ee" and move quickly into saying "uh" (eeuh, eeuh, eeuh).

Appendix B

<table>
<tr><th colspan="24">Index Of Practice Materials By Language</th></tr>
<tr><th rowspan="2">Language</th><th colspan="23">Chapter</th></tr>
<tr><th>1</th><th>2</th><th>3</th><th>4</th><th>5</th><th>6</th><th>7</th><th>8</th><th>9</th><th>10</th><th>11</th><th>12</th><th>13</th><th>14</th><th>15</th><th>16</th><th>17</th><th>18</th><th>19</th><th>20</th><th>21</th><th>22</th><th>23</th></tr>
<tr><td>Akan</td><td></td><td></td><td>√</td><td></td><td>√</td><td>√</td><td>√</td><td></td><td></td><td></td><td></td><td></td><td></td><td>√</td><td></td><td></td><td>√</td><td>√</td><td></td><td>√</td><td>√</td><td></td><td></td></tr>
<tr><td>Arabic</td><td>√</td><td></td><td>√</td><td></td><td></td><td></td><td>√</td><td>√</td><td></td><td></td><td>√</td><td></td><td>√</td><td>√</td><td></td><td>√</td><td></td><td></td><td></td><td>√</td><td>√</td><td>√</td><td></td></tr>
<tr><td>Berber</td><td>√</td><td></td><td>√</td><td></td><td></td><td></td><td>√</td><td></td><td></td><td></td><td></td><td></td><td></td><td></td><td>√</td><td>√</td><td>√</td><td></td><td></td><td></td><td>√</td><td></td><td></td></tr>
<tr><td>Bulgarian</td><td>√</td><td>√</td><td>√</td><td></td><td></td><td></td><td>√</td><td></td><td></td><td></td><td></td><td></td><td></td><td></td><td></td><td>√</td><td>√</td><td></td><td></td><td></td><td></td><td></td><td></td></tr>
<tr><td>Cantonese</td><td>√</td><td></td><td></td><td></td><td>√</td><td>√</td><td></td><td></td><td></td><td></td><td></td><td></td><td>√</td><td></td><td></td><td>√</td><td></td><td>√</td><td></td><td></td><td></td><td></td><td>√</td></tr>
<tr><td>Dutch</td><td>√</td><td></td><td></td><td></td><td></td><td></td><td></td><td></td><td></td><td>√</td><td></td><td></td><td></td><td></td><td></td><td>√</td><td></td><td></td><td></td><td></td><td></td><td></td><td></td></tr>
<tr><td>Ewe</td><td></td><td></td><td>√</td><td></td><td>√</td><td></td><td>√</td><td></td><td></td><td></td><td></td><td></td><td></td><td>√</td><td></td><td>√</td><td>√</td><td></td><td></td><td>√</td><td></td><td></td><td></td></tr>
<tr><td>Farsi</td><td>√</td><td></td><td>√</td><td></td><td>√</td><td>√</td><td></td><td></td><td>√</td><td>√</td><td></td><td></td><td></td><td>√</td><td></td><td>√</td><td>√</td><td></td><td></td><td>√</td><td></td><td></td><td></td></tr>
<tr><td>Finnish</td><td>√</td><td></td><td>√</td><td>√</td><td></td><td></td><td>√</td><td></td><td></td><td></td><td></td><td>√</td><td></td><td>√</td><td>√</td><td>√</td><td>√</td><td></td><td></td><td></td><td></td><td></td><td></td></tr>
<tr><td>French</td><td></td><td></td><td></td><td></td><td></td><td></td><td></td><td></td><td></td><td></td><td></td><td>√</td><td></td><td></td><td></td><td>√</td><td>√</td><td>√</td><td>√</td><td>√</td><td>√</td><td>√</td><td>√</td></tr>
<tr><td>German</td><td>√</td><td></td><td>√</td><td>√</td><td>√</td><td>√</td><td>√</td><td></td><td></td><td></td><td></td><td>√</td><td></td><td></td><td></td><td>√</td><td></td><td></td><td></td><td></td><td></td><td></td><td></td></tr>
<tr><td>Gujarati</td><td>√</td><td>√</td><td>√</td><td></td><td></td><td></td><td></td><td></td><td></td><td></td><td></td><td></td><td></td><td>√</td><td>√</td><td>√</td><td>√</td><td></td><td></td><td>√</td><td></td><td></td><td></td></tr>
<tr><td>Hindi</td><td>√</td><td></td><td>√</td><td></td><td></td><td></td><td></td><td></td><td></td><td></td><td></td><td></td><td></td><td></td><td></td><td>√</td><td>√</td><td></td><td></td><td></td><td></td><td></td><td></td></tr>
<tr><td>Hungarian</td><td>√</td><td></td><td>√</td><td></td><td>√</td><td></td><td></td><td></td><td></td><td></td><td></td><td></td><td></td><td></td><td>√</td><td>√</td><td></td><td>√</td><td></td><td></td><td></td><td>√</td><td></td></tr>
<tr><td>Indonesian</td><td>√</td><td></td><td>√</td><td></td><td></td><td></td><td></td><td></td><td></td><td></td><td></td><td></td><td></td><td></td><td></td><td>√</td><td>√</td><td>√</td><td></td><td></td><td></td><td></td><td></td></tr>
<tr><td>Italian</td><td>√</td><td></td><td></td><td></td><td>√</td><td>√</td><td></td><td></td><td>√</td><td></td><td></td><td></td><td></td><td>√</td><td>√</td><td>√</td><td></td><td></td><td></td><td></td><td></td><td>√</td><td></td></tr>
<tr><td>Japanese</td><td>√</td><td></td><td>√</td><td></td><td>√</td><td>√</td><td>√</td><td></td><td></td><td></td><td></td><td>√</td><td></td><td></td><td></td><td>√</td><td></td><td></td><td></td><td></td><td></td><td>√</td><td></td></tr>
<tr><td>Kannada</td><td>√</td><td>√</td><td>√</td><td>√</td><td>√</td><td>√</td><td>√</td><td></td><td></td><td></td><td></td><td></td><td></td><td></td><td></td><td>√</td><td></td><td></td><td></td><td></td><td>√</td><td></td><td></td></tr>
<tr><td>Korean</td><td>√</td><td></td><td>√</td><td></td><td>√</td><td>√</td><td>√</td><td></td><td></td><td></td><td></td><td></td><td></td><td>√</td><td>√</td><td>√</td><td>√</td><td>√</td><td>√</td><td>√</td><td>√</td><td></td><td></td></tr>
<tr><td>Malay</td><td>√</td><td>√</td><td>√</td><td></td><td>√</td><td>√</td><td>√</td><td></td><td></td><td></td><td></td><td></td><td></td><td>√</td><td>√</td><td>√</td><td>√</td><td></td><td></td><td></td><td></td><td></td><td></td></tr>
<tr><td>Mandarin</td><td>√</td><td></td><td>√</td><td>√</td><td>√</td><td>√</td><td>√</td><td></td><td></td><td></td><td></td><td></td><td></td><td>√</td><td>√</td><td>√</td><td>√</td><td>√</td><td>√</td><td>√</td><td>√</td><td>√</td><td>√</td></tr>
<tr><td>Marathi</td><td>√</td><td>√</td><td>√</td><td>√</td><td>√</td><td>√</td><td>√</td><td></td><td></td><td></td><td></td><td></td><td></td><td>√</td><td>√</td><td>√</td><td></td><td></td><td></td><td>√</td><td></td><td></td><td></td></tr>
<tr><td>Polish</td><td>√</td><td></td><td>√</td><td></td><td>√</td><td>√</td><td></td><td>√</td><td></td><td></td><td></td><td></td><td></td><td>√</td><td></td><td>√</td><td></td><td></td><td></td><td>√</td><td></td><td></td><td></td></tr>
<tr><td>Portuguese</td><td>√</td><td>√</td><td>√</td><td></td><td>√</td><td>√</td><td>√</td><td>√</td><td>√</td><td>√</td><td></td><td>√</td><td>√</td><td>√</td><td>√</td><td>√</td><td>√</td><td>√</td><td>√</td><td>√</td><td>√</td><td></td><td></td></tr>
<tr><td>Romanian</td><td>√</td><td></td><td>√</td><td></td><td>√</td><td>√</td><td>√</td><td></td><td></td><td></td><td></td><td></td><td></td><td>√</td><td>√</td><td>√</td><td></td><td></td><td></td><td>√</td><td></td><td></td><td></td></tr>
<tr><td>Russian</td><td>√</td><td></td><td>√</td><td></td><td>√</td><td>√</td><td>√</td><td></td><td></td><td></td><td></td><td></td><td></td><td>√</td><td></td><td>√</td><td>√</td><td></td><td>√</td><td></td><td>√</td><td></td><td></td></tr>
<tr><td>Rwandese</td><td>√</td><td></td><td>√</td><td></td><td>√</td><td>√</td><td>√</td><td></td><td></td><td></td><td>√</td><td></td><td>√</td><td></td><td>√</td><td>√</td><td>√</td><td></td><td></td><td>√</td><td></td><td></td><td>√</td></tr>
<tr><td>Serbian</td><td>√</td><td></td><td>√</td><td></td><td>√</td><td></td><td>√</td><td>√</td><td></td><td></td><td></td><td></td><td></td><td></td><td>√</td><td></td><td></td><td></td><td></td><td>√</td><td>√</td><td>√</td><td></td></tr>
<tr><td>Shona</td><td>√</td><td></td><td>√</td><td></td><td>√</td><td></td><td></td><td></td><td></td><td></td><td></td><td></td><td></td><td>√</td><td>√</td><td>√</td><td></td><td></td><td></td><td>√</td><td>√</td><td></td><td></td></tr>
<tr><td>Sinhala</td><td>√</td><td>√</td><td>√</td><td>√</td><td>√</td><td>√</td><td></td><td>√</td><td></td><td></td><td></td><td></td><td>√</td><td>√</td><td></td><td>√</td><td>√</td><td>√</td><td></td><td></td><td></td><td></td><td></td></tr>
<tr><td>Slovene</td><td></td><td></td><td>√</td><td></td><td></td><td>√</td><td>√</td><td></td><td></td><td></td><td></td><td></td><td></td><td></td><td></td><td></td><td></td><td></td><td></td><td></td><td></td><td></td><td></td></tr>
<tr><td>Spanish</td><td>√</td><td></td><td>√</td><td>√</td><td></td><td></td><td>√</td><td>√</td><td>√</td><td></td><td></td><td>√</td><td></td><td>√</td><td>√</td><td></td><td></td><td></td><td></td><td>√</td><td></td><td></td><td></td></tr>
<tr><td>Tagalog</td><td>√</td><td></td><td>√</td><td></td><td>√</td><td></td><td>√</td><td></td><td></td><td></td><td></td><td></td><td></td><td>√</td><td></td><td>√</td><td>√</td><td></td><td></td><td></td><td></td><td></td><td></td></tr>
<tr><td>Tamil</td><td>√</td><td>√</td><td>√</td><td>√</td><td>√</td><td>√</td><td>√</td><td></td><td>√</td><td></td><td>√</td><td></td><td></td><td>√</td><td>√</td><td></td><td></td><td></td><td></td><td>√</td><td></td><td></td><td></td></tr>
<tr><td>Telugu</td><td>√</td><td>√</td><td>√</td><td>√</td><td>√</td><td>√</td><td>√</td><td></td><td></td><td></td><td></td><td></td><td></td><td>√</td><td>√</td><td></td><td></td><td>√</td><td>√</td><td>√</td><td></td><td></td><td></td></tr>
<tr><td>Thai</td><td>√</td><td></td><td>√</td><td>√</td><td>√</td><td></td><td></td><td></td><td></td><td></td><td></td><td>√</td><td></td><td>√</td><td>√</td><td>√</td><td>√</td><td>√</td><td>√</td><td></td><td></td><td>√</td><td></td></tr>
<tr><td>Toruba</td><td>√</td><td></td><td>√</td><td></td><td>√</td><td>√</td><td>√</td><td></td><td></td><td>√</td><td></td><td>√</td><td></td><td></td><td>√</td><td>√</td><td>√</td><td></td><td></td><td>√</td><td></td><td></td><td></td></tr>
<tr><td>Turkish</td><td>√</td><td></td><td>√</td><td>√</td><td>√</td><td>√</td><td></td><td></td><td></td><td></td><td></td><td></td><td></td><td></td><td>√</td><td>√</td><td></td><td></td><td></td><td>√</td><td></td><td></td><td></td></tr>
<tr><td>Urdu</td><td>√</td><td>√</td><td>√</td><td></td><td>√</td><td>√</td><td>√</td><td>√</td><td>√</td><td></td><td></td><td></td><td>√</td><td>√</td><td>√</td><td></td><td>√</td><td></td><td></td><td></td><td></td><td></td><td></td></tr>
<tr><td>Vietnamese</td><td>√</td><td></td><td>√</td><td></td><td>√</td><td>√</td><td>√</td><td>√</td><td></td><td></td><td></td><td></td><td>√</td><td></td><td>√</td><td>√</td><td>√</td><td></td><td>√</td><td></td><td></td><td></td><td>√</td></tr>
</table>

Appendix C

A Glossary of Terms Used in Speech Science

1. **affricate**: a fricative speech sound initiated by a plosive. An example is /ch/.

2. **articulation**: the production of individual sounds in connected discourse; the movement and placement during speech of the organs which serve to interrupt or modify the voiced or unvoiced air stream into meaningful sounds; the speech function performed largely through the movements of the **lower jaw, lips, tongue, and soft palate**.

3. **bilabial**: used to describe a consonant sound formed with the aid of both lips.

4. **consonant**: a speech sound produced, with or without laryngeal vibration, by certain successive contractions of the articulatory muscles which modify, interrupt, or obstruct the expired air stream to the extent that its pressure is raised.

5. **diaphragm**: the muscular and tendonous partition which separates the abdominal and thoracic cavities; the chief muscle in breathing.

6. **diphthong**: a speech sound gliding continuously from one vowel to another in the same syllable such as /au/, /oi/, and /ai/.

7. **foreign accent**: the influence of speech sounds of a native language on those of a later learned second language.

8. **fricative**: any speech sound produced by forcing an air stream through a narrow opening and resulting in audible high-frequency vibrations.

9. **glottis**: the opening between the vocal cords.

10. **hard palate**: the bony roof of the mouth.

11. **homophone**: a word pronounced the same as another but different in meaning

12. **labial**: pertaining to the lips; a speech sound produced with the aid of the lips.

13. **labiodental**: a speech sound produced by the contact of the lips with the teeth.

14. **larynx**: the cartilaginous and muscular structure situated at the top of the trachea and below the tongue roots and hyoid bone; the organ of voice consisting of nine cartilages connected by ligaments.

15. **linguadental**: a speech sound produced with the aid of the tongue and teeth.

16. **lingual**: pertaining to the tongue.

17. **medial**: pertaining to the middle.

18. **nasal**: pertaining to the nose; also a voiced continuant speech sound having nasal resonance as its distinctive acoustic characteristic.

19. **palatogram**: an imprint on a thin, artificial hard palate made by contact of the tongue when a given sound is produced.

20. **phonation**: the production of voiced sound by means of vocal cord vibrations.

21. **phoneme**: a speech sound.

22. **phonetics**: the study of the production and perception of speech sounds including individual and group variations as to their use in speech.

23. **phonics**: the study of speech sounds with special reference to reading.

24. **phrase**: a group of words uttered without perceptible pause and set aside as a group by pauses of sufficient duration to perform this function.

25. **plosive**: any speech sound made by creating air pressure in the air tract and suddenly releasing it.

26. **quality**: when applied to voice, the acoustic characteristics of vowels resulting from their overtone structure or the relative intensities of their frequency components.

27. **resonance**: the vibratory response of a body or air-filled cavity to a frequency imposed upon it.

28. **semantics**: the study of the history and evolution of word meanings.

29. **sibilant**: a hissing sound; especially a type of fricative speech sound. Examples are /s/, /z/, and /ʃ/.

30. **soft palate**: a moveable fibromuscular sheet which is attached to the back margin of the hard palate; it helps to separate the oral cavity from the back wall of the mouth and, when elevated, closes off the oral from the nasal cavity.

31. **speech discrimination**: the ability to hear and recognize differences among all the sounds in speech segments.

32. **stop**: a speech sound produced when the air stream is blocked.

33. **trachea**: the windpipe; the cartilaginous and membranous tube descending from the larynx to the bronchi.

34. **uvula**: the appendage which hangs from the free margin of the soft palate.

35. **voice**: sound produced by the vibration of the vocal cord

36. **vowel**: a vocal sound produced by positions of the speech organs which offer little obstruction to the air stream and which form a series of resonators above the level of the larynx in the vocal tract.

37. **vowel glide**: a speech sound in which the speech mechanism moves from the position for one vowel to that of another without interruption and accompanied by continuous voicing . Examples are /ai/ and /ei/.

Appendix D

1,000 most frequently used words in English

1.the	50. she	99. now	148. too	197. build
2.of	51. which	100. find	149. same	198. self
3. to	52. do	101. any	150. tell	199. earth
4. and	53. their	102. new	151. does	200. father
5. a	54. time	103. work	152. set	201. head
6. in	55. if	104. part	153. three	202. stand
7. is	56. will	105. take	154. want	203. own
8. it	57. way	106. get	155. air	204. page
9. you	58. about	107. place	156. well	205. should
10. that	59. many	108. made	157. also	206. country
11. he	60. then	109. live	158. play	207. found
12. was	61. them	110. where	159. small	208. answer
13. for	62. write	111. after	160. end	209. school
14. on	63. would	112. back	161. put	210. grow
15. are	64. like	113. little	162. home	211. study
16. with	65. so	114. only	163. read	212. still
17. as	66. these	115. round	164. hand	213. learn
18. I	67. her	116. man	165. port	214. plant
19. his	68. long	117. year	166. large	215. cover
20. they	69. make	118. came	167. spell	216. food
21. be	70. thing	119. show	168. add	217. sun
22. at	71. see	120. every	169. even	218. four
23. one	72. him	121. good	170. land	219. between
24. have	73. two	122. me	171. here	220. state
25. this	74. has	123. give	172. must	221. keep
26. from	75. look	124. our	173. big	222. eye
27. or	76. more	125. under	174. high	223. never
28. had	77. day.	126. name	175. such	224. last
29. by	78. could	127. very	176. follow	225. let
30. hot	79. go	128. through	177. act	226. thought
31. word	80. come	129. just	178. why	227. city
32. but	81. did	130. form	179. ask	228. tree
33. what	82. number	131. sentence	180. men	229. cross
34. some	83. sound	132. great	181. change	230. farm
35. we	84. no	133. think	182. went	231. hard
36. can	85. most	134. say	183. light	232. start
37. out	86. people	135. help	184. kind	233. might
38. other	87. my	136. low	185. off	234. story
39. were	88. over	137. line	186. need	235. saw
40. all	89. know	138. differ	187. house	236. far
41. there	90. water	139. turn	188. picture	237. sea
42. when	91. than	140. cause	189. try	238. draw
43. up	92. call	141. much	190. us	239. left
44. use	93. first	142. mean	191. again	240. late
45. your	94. who	143. before	192. animal	241. run
46. how	95. may	144. move	193. point	242. don't
47. said	96. down	145. right	194. mother	243. while
48. an	97. side	146. boy	195. world	244. press
49. each	98. been	147. old	196. near	245. close

246. night
247. real
248. life
249. few
250. north
251. open
252. seem
253. together
254. next
255. white
256. children
257. begin
258. got
259. walk
260. example
261. ease
262. paper
263. group
264. always
265. music
266. those
267. both
268. mark
269. often
270. letter
271. until
272. mile
273. river
274. car
275. feet
276. care
277. second
278. book
279. carry
280. took
281. science
282. eat
283. room
284. friend
285. began
286. idea
287. fish
288. mountain
289. stop
290. once
291. base
292. hear
293. horse
294. cut
295. sure
296. watch
297. color
298. face
299. wood

300. main
301. enough
302. plain
303. girl
304. usual
305. young
306. ready
307. above
308. ever
309. red
310. list
311. though
312. feel
313. talk
314. bird
315. soon
316. body
317. dog
318. family
319. direct
320. pose
321. leave
322. song
323. measure
324. door
325. product
326. black
327. short
328. numeral
329. class
330. wind
331. question
332. happen
333. complete
334. ship
335. area
336. half
337. rock
338. order
339. fire
340. south
341. problem
342. piece
343. told
344. knew
345. pass
346. since
347. top
348. whole
349. king
350. space
351. heard
352. best
353. hour

354. better
355. true
356. during
357. hundred
358. five
359. remember
360. step
361. early
362. hold
363. west
364. ground
365. interest
366. reach
367. fast
368. verb
369. sing
370. listen
371. six
372. table
373. travel
374. less
375. morning
376. ten
377. simple
378. several
379. vowel
380. toward
381. war
382. lay
383. against
384. pattern
385. slow
386. center
387. love
388. person
389. money
390. serve
391. appear
392. road
393. map
394. rain
395. rule
396. govern
397. pull
398. cold
399. notice
400. voice
401. unit
402. power
403. town
404. fine
405. certain
406. fly
407. fall

408. lead
409. cry
410. dark
411. machine
412. note
413. wait
414. plan
415. figure
416. star
417. box
418. noun
419. field
420. rest
421. correct
422. able
423. pound
424. done
425. beauty
426. drive
427. stood
428. contain
429. front
430. teach
431. week
432. final
433. gave
434. green
435. oh
436. quick
437. develop
438. ocean
439. warm
440. free
441. minute
442. strong
443. special
444. mind
445. behind
446. mind
447. tail
448. produce
449. fact
450. street
451. inch
452. multiply
453. nothing
454. course
455. stay
456. wheel
457. full
458. force
459. blue
460. object
461. decide

462. surface
463. deep
464. moon
465. island
466. foot
467. system
468. busy
469. test
470. record
471. boat
472. common
473. gold
474. possible
475. plane
476. stead
477. dry
478. wonder
479. laugh
480. thousand
481. ago
482. ran
483. check
484. game
485. shape
486. equate
487. hot
488. miss
489. brought
490. heat
491. snow
492. tire
493. bring
494. yes
495. distant
496. fill
497. east
498. paint
499. language
500. street
501. grand
502. ball
503. yet
504. wave
505. drop
506. heart
507. am
508. present
509. heavy
510. dance
511. engine
512. position
513. arm
514. wide
515. sail

516. material	570. joy	624. hill	678. cloud	732. team
517. size	571. winter	625. safe	679. surprise	733. wire
518. vary	572. sat	626. cat	680. quiet	734. cost
519. settle	573. written	627. century	681. stone	735. lost
520. speak	574. wild	628. consider	682. tiny	736. brown
521. weight	575. instrument	629. type	683. climb	737. wear
522. general	576. kept	630. law	684. cool	738. garden
523. ice	577. glass	631. bit	685. design	739. equal
524. matter	578. grass	632. coast	686. poor	740. sent
525. circle	579. cow	633. copy	687. lot	741. choose
526. pair	580. job	634. phrase	688. experiment	742. fell
527. include	581. edge	635. silent	689. bottom	743. fit
528. divide	582. sign	636. tall	690. key	744. how
529. syllable	583. visit	637. sand	691. iron	745. fair
530. felt	584. past	638. soil	692. single	746. bank
531. perhaps	585. soft	639. roll	693. stick	747. collect
532. pick	586. fun	640. temperature	694. flat	748. save
533. sudden	587. bright	641. finger	695. twenty	749. control
534. count	588. gas	642. industry	696. skin	750. decimal
535. square	589. weather	643. value	697. smile	751. gentle
536. reason	590. month	644. fight	698. crease	752. woman
537. length	591. million	645. lie	699. hole	753. captain
538. represent	592. bear	646. beat	700. trade	754. practice
539. art	593. finish	647. excite	701. melody	755. separate
540. subject	594. happy	648. natural	702. trip	756. difficult
541. region	595. hope	649. view	703. office	757. doctor
542. energy	596. flower	650. sense	704. receive	758. please
543. hunt	597. clothe	651. ear	705. row	759. protect
544. probable	598. strange	652. else	706. mouth	760. noon
545. bed	599. gone	653. quite	707. exact	761. whose
546. brother	600. jump	654. broke	708. symbol	762. locate
547. egg	601. baby	655. case	709. die	763. ring
548. ride	602. eight	656. middle	710. least	764. character
549. cell	603. village	657. kill	711. trouble	765. insect
550. believe	604. meet	658. son	712. shout	766. caught
551. fraction	605. root	659. lake	713. except	767. period
552. forest	606. buy	660. moment	714. wrote	768. indicate
553. sit	607. raise	661. scale	715. seed	769. radio
554. race	608. solve	662. loud	716. tone	770. spoke
555. window	609. metal	663. spring	717. join	771. atom
556. store	610. whether	664. observe	718. suggest	772. human
557. summer	611. push	665. child	719. clean	773. history
558. train	612. seven	666. straight	720. break	774. effect
559. sleep	613. paragraph	667. consonant	721. lady	775. electric
560. prove	614. third	668. nation	722. yard	776. expect
561. lone	615. small	669. dictionary	723. rise	777. crop
562. leg	616. held	670. milk	724. bad	778. modern
563. exercise	617. hair	671. speed	725. blow	779. element
564. wall	618. describe	672. method	726. oil	780. hit
565. catch	619. cook	673. organ	727. blood	781. student
566. mount	620. floor	674. pay	728. touch	782. corner
567. wish	621. either	675. age	729. grew	783. party
568. sky	622. result	676. section	730. cent	784. supply
569. board	623. burn	677. dress	731. mix	785. bone

786. rail	840. gun	894. prepare	948. double
787. imagine	841. allow	895. salt	949. seat
788. provide	842. print	896. nose	950. arrive
789. agree	843. dead	897. plural	951. master
790. thus	844. spot	898. anger	952. track
791. capital	845. desert	899. claim	953. parent
792. won't	846. suit	900. continent	954. shore
793. chair	847. current	901. oxygen	955. division
794. danger	848. lift	902. sugar	956. sheet
795. fruit	849. rose	903. death	957. substance
796. rich	850. continue	904. pretty	958. favor
797. thick	851. block	905. skill	959. connect
798. soldier	852. chart	906. women	960. post
799. process	853. hat	907. season	961. spend
800. operate	854. sell	908. solution	962. chord
801. guess	855. success	909. magnet	963. fat
802. necessary	856. company	910. silver	964. glad
803. sharp	857. subtract	911. thank	965. original
804. wing	858. event	912. branch	966. share
805. create	859. particular	913. match	967. station
806. neighbor	860. deal	914. suffix	968. dad
807. wash	861. swim	915. especial	969. bread
808. bat	862. term	916. fig	970. charge
809. rather	863. opposite	917. afraid	971. proper
810. crowd	864. wife	918. huge	972. bar
811. corn	865. shoe	919. sister	973. offer
812. compare	866. shoulder	920. steel	974. segment
813. poem	867. spread	921. discuss	975. slave
814. string	868. arrange	922. forward	976. duck
815. bell	869. camp	923. similar	977. instant
816. depend	870. invent	924. guide	978. market
817. meat	871. cotton	925. experience	979. degree
818. rub	872. born	926. score	980. populate
819. tube	873. determine	927. apple	981. chick
820. famous	874. quart	928. bought	982. dear
821. dollar	875. nine	929. led	983. enemy
822. stream	876. truck	930. pitch	984. reply
823. fear	877. noise	931. coat	985. drink
824. sight	878. level	932. mass	986. occur
825. thin	879. chance	933. card	987. support
826. triangle	880. gather	934. band	988. speech
827. planet	881. shop	935. rope	989. nature
828. hurry	882. stretch	936. slip	990. range
829. chief	883. throw	937. win	991. steam
830. colony	884. shine	938. dream	992. motion
831. clock	885. property	939. evening	993. path
832. mine	886. column	940. condition	994. liquid
833. tie	887. molecule	941. feed	995. log
834. enter	888. select	942. tool	996. meant
835. major	889. wrong	943. total	997. quotient
836. fresh	890. gray	944. basic	998. teeth
837. search	891. repeat	945. smell	999. shall
838. send	892. require	946. valley	1000. neck
839. yellow	893. broad	947. nor	

Suggested Resources

1. <u>Dictionary of Prepositions for Students of English</u>, by Eugene J. Hall. Copyright 1982, ISBN 0-8056-0114-7

2. <u>Biz Talk-1 American Business Slang and Jargon</u>, by David Burke. Copyright 1993, ISBN 9 781879 440173

3. <u>Random House Webster's Dictionary of American English</u> copyright 1997, ISBN 0-679-76425-9

4. <u>Random House Webster's English Language Desk Reference</u> copyright 1997 ISBN 0-679-78000-9

5. <u>NTC's Dictionary of Everyday American English Expressions</u>, by Spears, Birner, and Kleinedler. Copyright 1994 ISBN 0-8442-5779-6

6. <u>NTC's Thematic Dictionary of American Idioms</u>, by Richard A. Spears, Ph.D, copyright 1997. ISBN 0-8442-0831-0

7. <u>NTC's Dictionary of American Slang and Colloquial Expressions</u>, Second Edition by Richard A. Spears, Ph.D. copyright 1995. ISBN 0-8442-0827-2

8. <u>NBC Handbook of Pronunciation</u>, by Ehrlich and Hand, copyright1991. ISBN 0-06-273056-8

9. <u>Barron's 1001 Pitfalls in English Grammar</u>, third edition by Craig and Hopper, copyright 1986. ISBN 0-8120-3719-7

10. <u>Edit Yourself: A Manual For Everyone Who Works With Words</u>, by Bruce Ross-Larson, copyright 1982 ISBN 0-393-01640-4

11. <u>Dr. Grammar's Writes From Wrongs</u> by Richard Francis Tracz. Copyright 1991. ISBN 0-679-72715-9

12. <u>BusinessSpeak: 4,000 Business Terms, Buzzwords, Acronyms, and Technical Words: All You Need to Say to Get Ahead in Corporate America</u>, by Schaaf and Kaeter. Copyright 1994. ISBN 0-446-36314-6

13. <u>The Big Book Of Beastly Mispronunciations</u> by Charles Harrington Elster. Copyright 1999. ISBN 0-395-89338-0

14. <u>The Chicago Manual of Style</u>. My copy is the 13th edition, copyright 1982, ISBN0-226-10390-0. The 14th edition is now in print.

15. <u>The Story of English</u>—A Companion to the PBS Television Series—which is also available on videocassette. Copyright 1986. ISBN 0-670-80467-3

16. <u>The Mother Tongue: English & How It Got That Way by Bill Bryson</u>. Copyright 1990, ISBN 0-688-07895-8

17. <u>Bryson's Dictionary of Troublesome Words</u> by Bill Bryson. Copyright 2002, ISBN 0-7679-1042-7

18. <u>A Pocket Reference to American English Grammar, Punctuation and Usage</u> by Linda A. Sikorski. Copyright 1988, ISBN: 1-883574-06-4

19. www.m-w.com A great online dictionary with clear sound. Type in your word and hear the pronunciation.

20. http://geocities.com/Athens/8136/tonguetwisters.html I used this website for most of the tongue twisters selected for use in this book.

21. http://owl.english.purdue.edu.owl This is my favorite website for English grammar and writing concerns. The owl stands for Online Writing Lab.

22. http://earlham.edu/~peters/writing/homofone.htm This one is my favorite website for homophones.

23. www.accent-professional.com This is my website. Please visit often!